WORLD ATL

How to Use Your SD-X Reader with This Book

This highly interactive book lets you explore the world in an interactive format. You can read the book and study the maps, photographs, and illustrations, but a touch of the SD-X Reader adds in-depth audio information, word definitions, and learning games to the pictures and maps.

1. Press the Power button to turn the SD-X Reader on or off. The LED will light up when the SD-X Reader is on.

2. Touch the volume buttons found on this page or on the Table of Contents page to adjust the volume.

3. Touch photographs, maps, and illustrations with the SD-X Reader to hear additional information. In a block of text, touch words that are a different color or size to hear a definition or more information.

4. As you touch around the page, you'll encounter games and quizzes. Touch the header or image that started the game to stop playing the game.

5. After two minutes of inactivity, the Reader will beep and go to sleep.

6. If the batteries are low, the Reader will beep twice and the LED will start blinking. Replace the batteries by following the instructions on the next page. The SD-X Reader uses two AAA batteries.

7. To use headphones or earbuds, plug them into the headphone jack on the bottom of the SD-X Reader.

CHANGE THE VOLUME WITH THESE BUTTONS

UP DOWN

Battery Information
Interactive Pen includes 2 replaceable AAA batteries (UM-4 or LR03).

Battery Installation
1. Open battery door with small flat-head or Phillips screwdriver.
2. Install new batteries according to +/- polarity. If batteries are not installed properly, the device will not function.
3. Replace battery door; secure with small screw.

Battery Safety
Batteries must be replaced by adults only. Properly dispose of used batteries. Do not dispose of batteries in fire; batteries may explode or leak. See battery manufacturer for disposal recommendations. Do not mix alkaline, standard (carbon-zinc), or rechargeable (nickel-cadmium) batteries. Do not mix old and new batteries. Only recommended batteries of the same or equivalent type should be used. Remove weakened or dead batteries. Never short-circuit the supply terminals. Non-rechargeable batteries are not to be recharged. Do not use rechargeable batteries. If batteries are swallowed, in the USA, promptly see a doctor and have the doctor phone 1-202-625-3333 collect. In other countries, have the doctor call your local poison control center. Batteries should be changed when sounds mix, distort, or become otherwise unintelligible as batteries weaken. The electrostatic discharge may interfere with the sound module. If this occurs, please simply restart the product.

In Europe, the dustbin symbol indicates that batteries, rechargeable batteries, button cells, battery packs, and similar materials must not be discarded in household waste. Batteries containing hazardous substances are harmful to the environment and to health. Please help to protect the environment from health risks by telling your children to dispose of batteries properly and by taking batteries to local collection points. Batteries handled in this manner are safely recycled.

Warning: Changes or modifications to this unit not expressly approved by the party responsible for compliance could void the user's authority to operate the equipment.

NOTE: This equipment has been tested and found to comply with the limits for a Class B digital device, pursuant to Part 15 of the FCC Rules. These limits are designed to provide reasonable protection against harmful interference in a residential installation. This equipment generates, uses, and can radiate radio frequency energy and, if not installed and used in accordance with the instructions, may cause harmful interference to radio communications. However, there is no guarantee that interference will not occur in a particular installation. If this equipment does cause harmful interference to radio or television reception, which can be determined by turning the equipment off and on, the user is encouraged to try to correct the interference by one or more of the following measures: Reorient or relocate the receiving antenna. Increase the separation between the equipment and receiver. Connect the equipment into an outlet on a circuit different from that to which the receiver is connected. Consult the dealer or an experienced radio TV technician for help.

Cover art from Shutterstock.com.

Interior art from Encyclopædia Britannica, Inc.; Getty Images; and Shutterstock.com. Page 4 art from Library of Congress, Geography and Map Division.

Louis Weber, CEO
Publications International, Ltd.
7373 North Cicero Avenue
Lincolnwood, Illinois 60712

Publications International, Ltd.

Customer Service
customer_service@pubint.com

ISBN: 978-1-4508-8408-2

Manufactured in China.

8 7 6 5 4 3 2 1

CONTENTS

CHANGE THE VOLUME WITH THESE BUTTONS

UP DOWN

INTRODUCTION

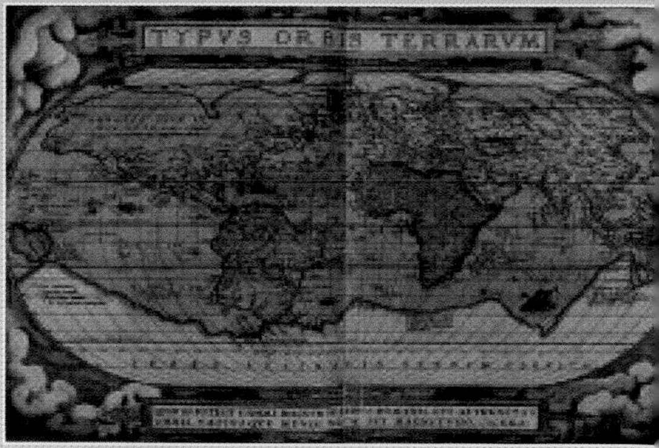

The study of the surface of Earth is called geography. Basic to the study of geography are two important considerations. These are the location of specific places or things and the patterns formed by the distribution of similar places or things over Earth. Geography is concerned not only with the distribution over the face of Earth of physical things but also with the arrangement of people and their activities.

There are many kinds of maps:

political maps
physical maps
thematic maps

WHERE DOES THE TERM "ATLAS" COME FROM?

A person who makes maps is called a cartographer.

WHAT DO YOU **KNOW?**

YES **NO**

A system of lines is used to find the location of any place on the surface of the Earth. Commonly called a grid system, it is made up of two sets of lines that cross each other. One set—lines of latitude—runs in an east-west direction. The other set—lines of longitude—runs in a north-south direction.

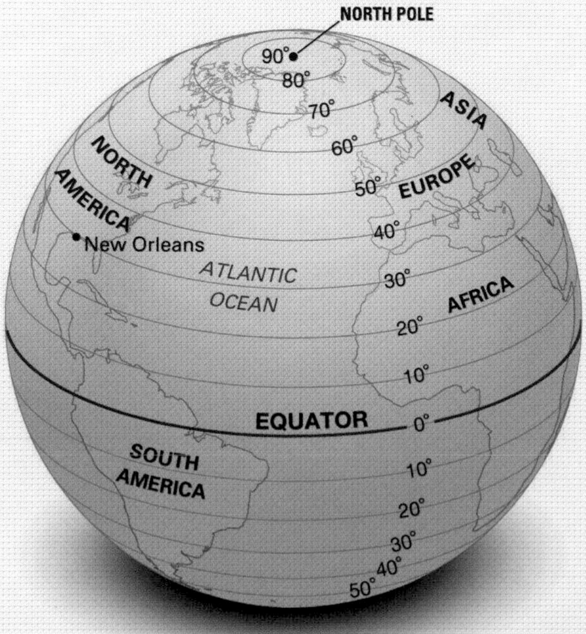

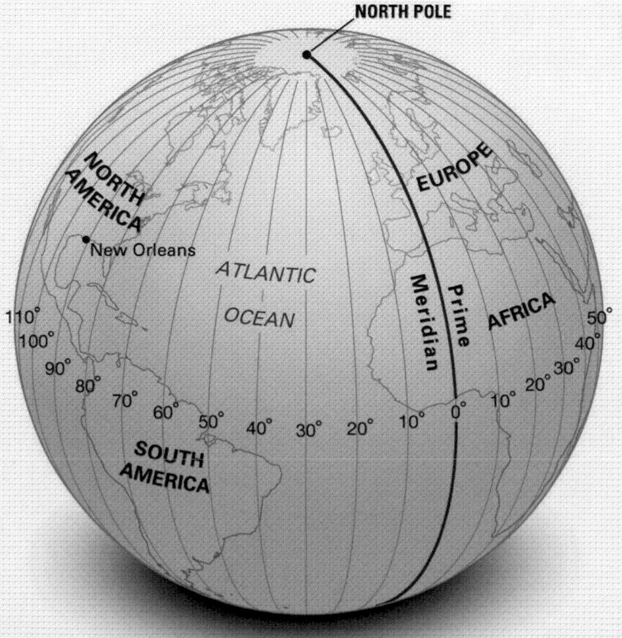

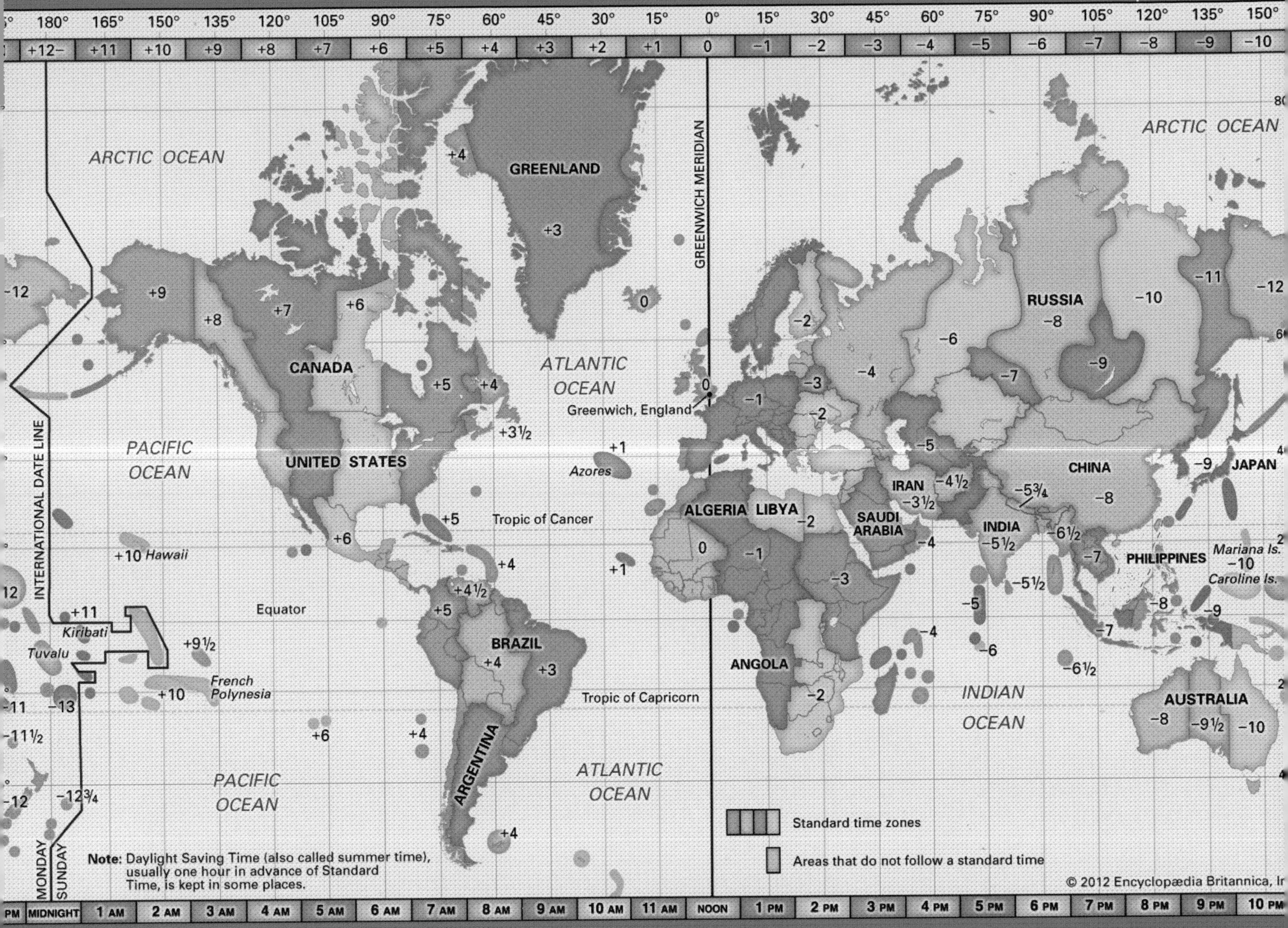

The world is divided into 24 time zones, each of which represents one hour of time.

The Earth resembles a sphere. A sphere can be imagined to be cut in half either horizontally or vertically. Half-spheres, or hemispheres, are the result.

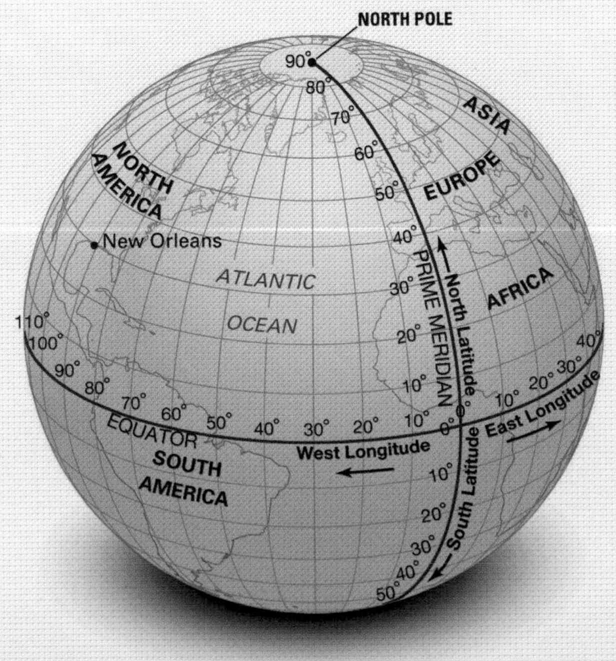

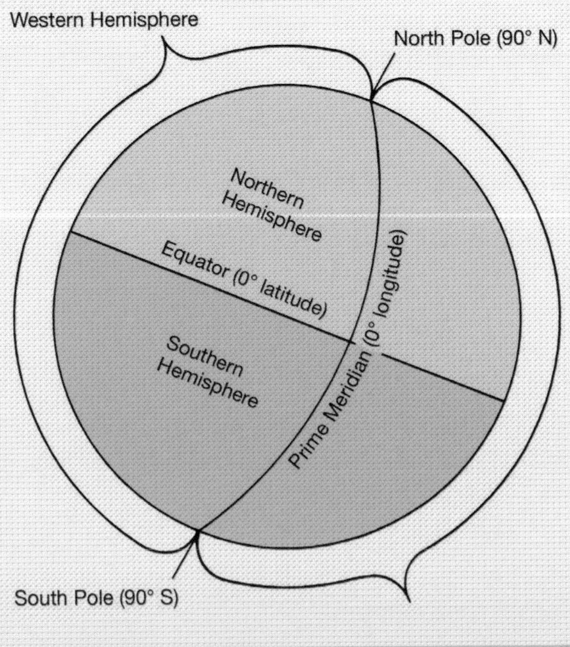

THE PHYSICAL WORLD

The continents are the large masses of land that stand above the level of the sea. Together they occupy only about 29 percent of Earth's surface. Earth's surface can be described as being rough or smooth. The rough lands include the world's mountains and hilly uplands. The flat lands are its **PLATEAUS** and plains. Each continent has its individual arrangement of landforms.

TRUE OR FALSE?
T F

NATURAL VEGETATION

Natural vegetation varies according to temperature, rainfall, soil, land surface, and other conditions. To date, more than 300,000 plant species have been identified and described. However, botanists estimate that there are tens of thousands of unidentified species yet to be discovered.

What type of trees are shown in the photograph?

THE OCEANS

The large continuous bodies of water that cover Earth are broken into irregular parts by continents and islands and are known as the oceans. Four are commonly recognized—the Pacific, Atlantic, Indian, and Arctic. Together, with their gulfs, bays, and seas, they make up about 71 percent of Earth's surface.

WHICH OCEAN IS LARGEST?

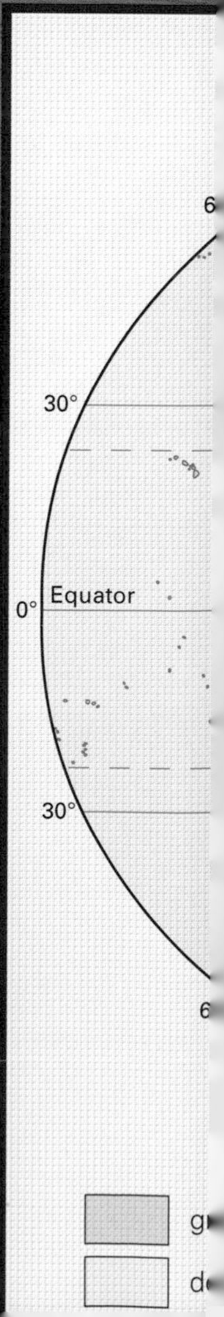

WHICH RIVER IS EARTH'S LONGEST?

ELEVATION

The highest point on Earth is the summit of Mount Everest, which lies at an elevation of 29,035 feet (8,850 meters).

Earth's lowest point on land

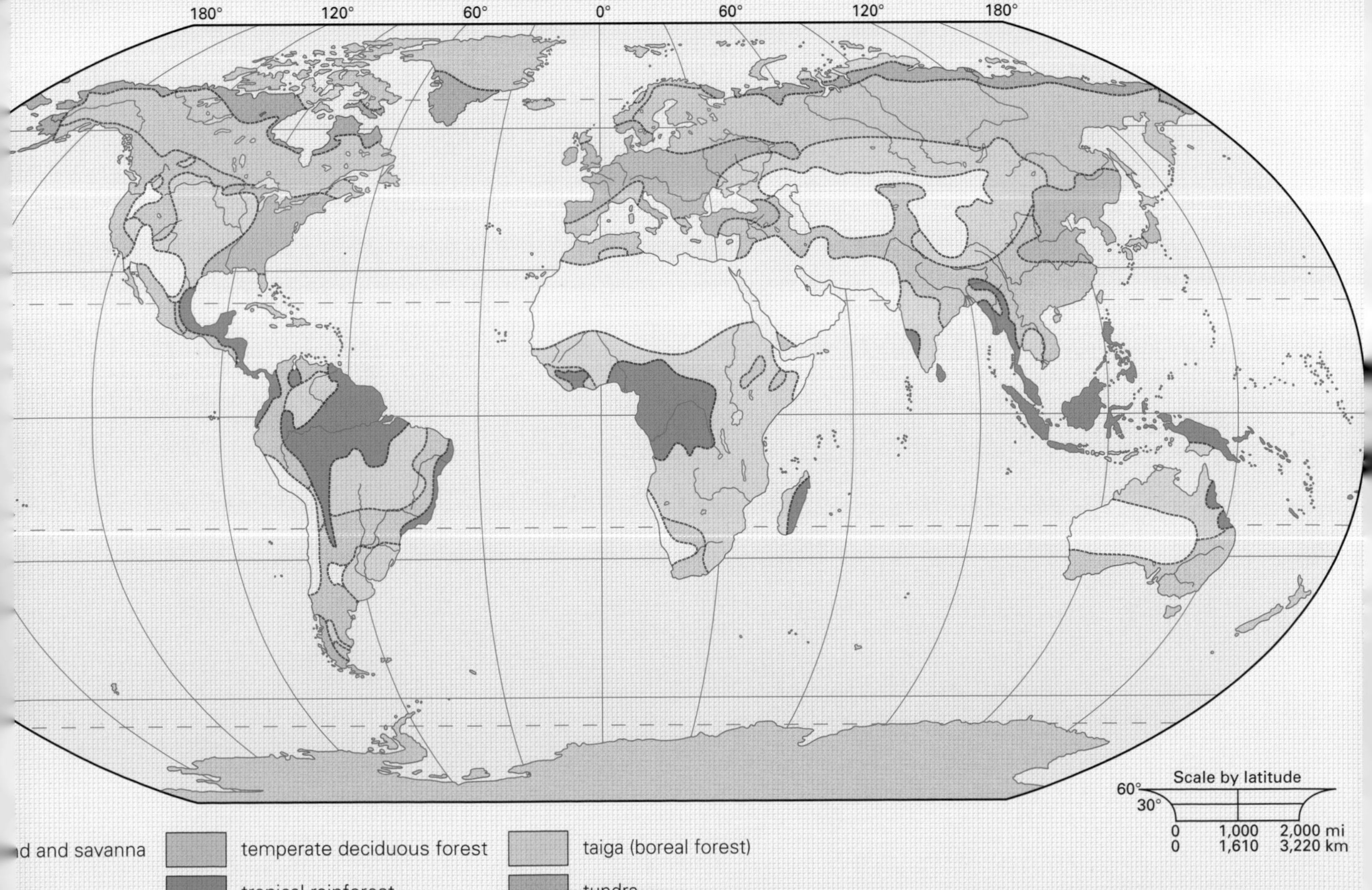

BIOMES

FIND THE BIOME.

A biome is the largest geographic unit made up of one major established or developing community of plants and animals with similar life-forms and environmental needs. At least six major terrestrial biomes are generally recognized (plus the marine and freshwater biomes).

Biomes are also called major life zones.

GRASSLAND & SAVANNA

In temperate or tropical regions where precipitation is sparse or erratic, grasses are the dominant plants. Trees and shrubs are rare or absent in **temperate grasslands**. Tropical grasslands, or **savannas**, have scattered drought-resistant trees.

TAIGA, OR BOREAL FOREST

The taiga covers a broad region of cold, but not permanently frozen, land south of the tundra. The taiga is warmer than the tundra and also receives more precipitation, mostly in summer.

DESERT

Many people associate deserts with intense heat, but these biomes actually are characterized by their extreme dryness. Deserts typically receive less than 10 inches (25 centimeters) of rain annually.

TROPICAL RAINFOREST

Lush with broad-leaved evergreen trees and diverse plant and animal life, tropical rainforests are situated in the wet, warm areas near the Equator.

TEMPERATE DECIDUOUS FOREST

In some of the milder climates of the Northern Hemisphere, temperate deciduous forests grow. They are found mainly in the temperate regions of eastern North America, western and central Europe, and eastern Asia.

TUNDRA

The coldest of the six major biomes, and one of the driest, is the tundra of the Arctic regions.

CLIMATE

The weather found in a certain place over a long period of time is known as the climate. For example, a description of weather might be "It rained yesterday in Phoenix," while "Phoenix gets only 10 inches of rain per year" would be a statement about climate. Descriptions of climate include such weather elements as temperature, precipitation, humidity, wind, cloudiness, and snow cover.

WAS THE SAHARA REGION ALWAYS A DESERT? **TOUCH TO FIND OUT!**

What controls the CLIMATE?

latitude

land and water distribution

prevailing winds and pressure belts

ocean currents

altitude

topography

clouds

cyclonic activity

CLIMATE CAN CHANGE

While "climate" is intended as a long-term description of weather, there remains the question of just how long a period it should describe. If one adopts a period such as 30 years, one can then describe changes in climate over longer periods, such as thousands or millions of years. Evidence of climate changes includes data from rocks and fossils, tree rings, and lake bed sediments, and human historical records. There is currently widespread concern about a rapid phase of climate change, commonly known as global warming.

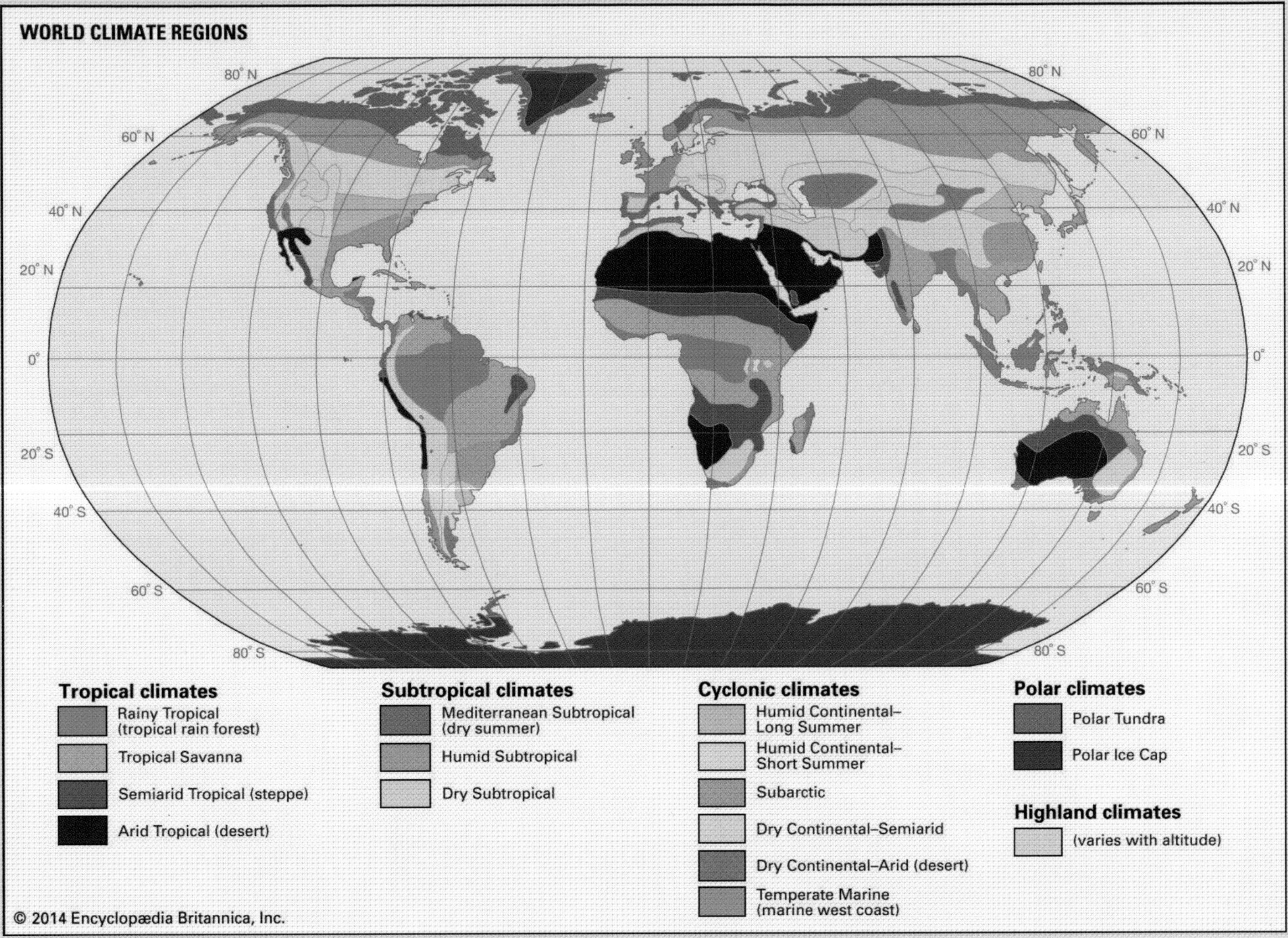

FIND A PLACE

AFRICA
ANTARCTICA
ASIA
EUROPE
NORTH AMERICA
SOUTH AMERICA
AUSTRALIA

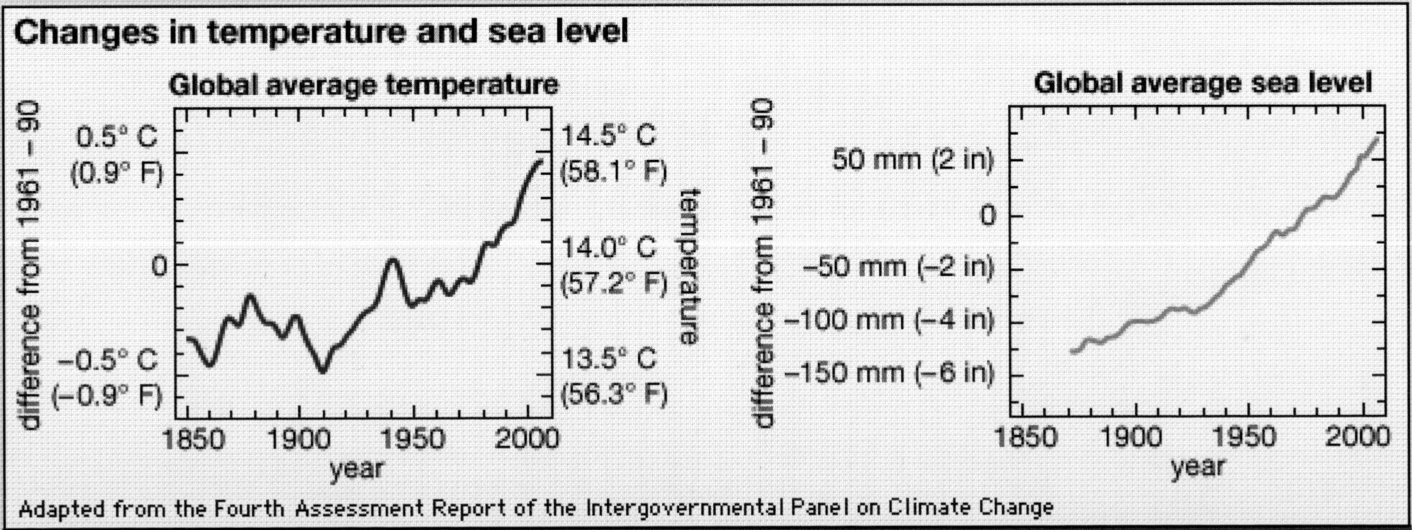

Data collected since the mid-1800s show increases in global average temperature and sea level.

EARTH'S GEOLOGY

The theory of plate tectonics says that Earth's outer layer is made up of large, moving pieces called plates. All of Earth's land and water sit on these plates. The plates are made of solid rock. Under the plates is a weaker layer of partially melted rock. The plates are constantly moving over this weaker layer.

How much do the tectonic plates move?

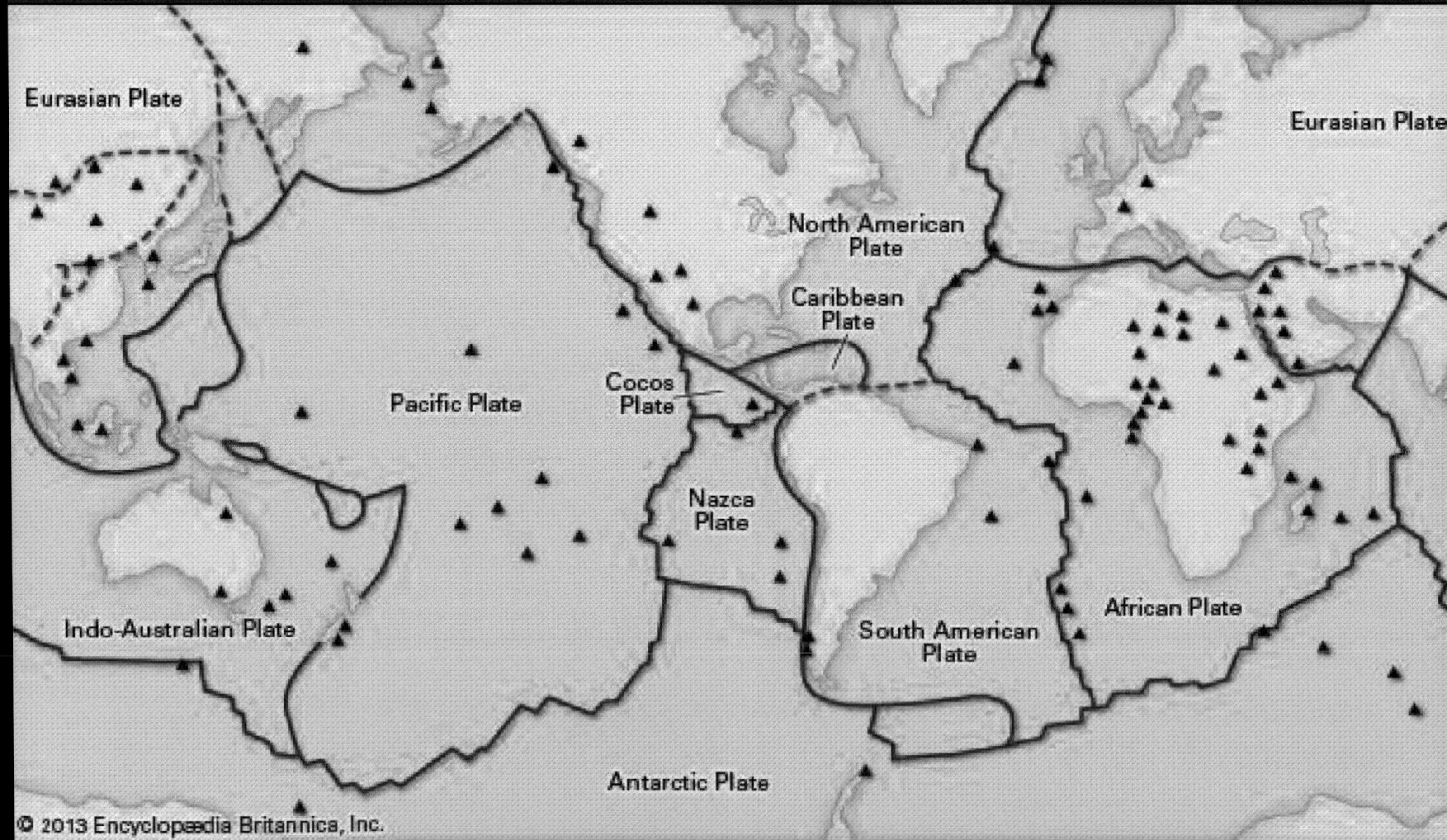

Divergence can happen on continents, producing fractures called rift valleys. Over millions of years the continental crust may separate completely, with the area between flooding with water to become a new ocean.

Two blocks of continental crust may **converge.** The resulting pressure can deform the crust. If one block is denser, that block may slide under the other, mainly lifting the other plate rather than sinking too much itself.

In some places, plates slide past each other laterally along fractures in the crust. These places are called transform faults. The plates stick and then occasionally slip, producing earthquakes.

ROCK FORMATION

Earth is largely a ball of rock. Rocks form on and beneath Earth's surface under a wide range of physical and chemical conditions. There are **IGNEOUS**, **METAMORPHIC**, and **SEDIMENTARY** rocks.

POLITICAL MAP

A nation is a unified territorial state with a political system that governs the whole society. A nation may be very large with several political subdivisions—such as the United States, China, Canada, or Australia—or it may be a small unit like the city-state of Singapore. A nation need not consist of a single, continuous geographical unit. The Philippines and Indonesia, for example, are made up of thousands of islands.

IS IT A COUNTRY?

YES NO

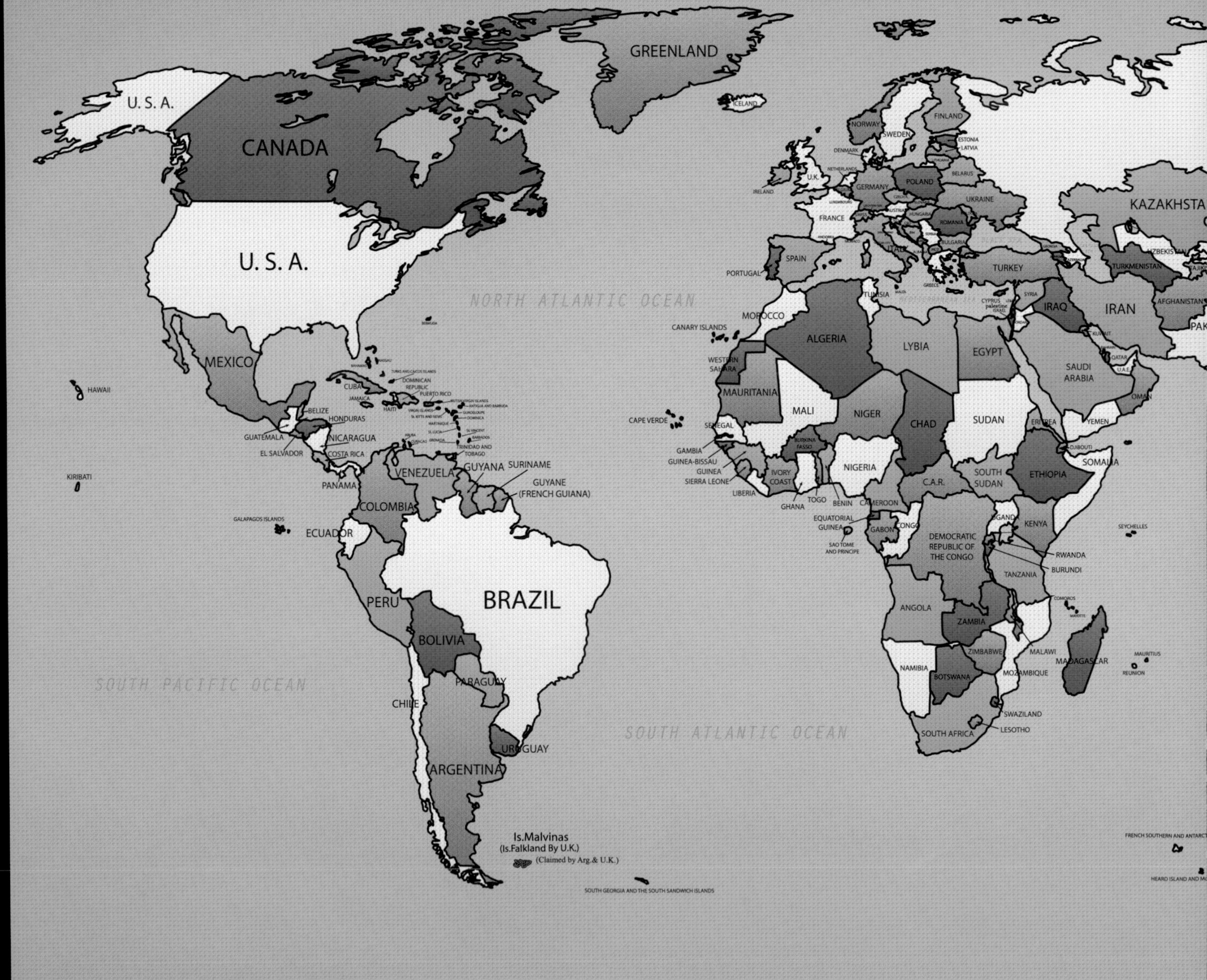

OF THE WORLD

Country Comparison

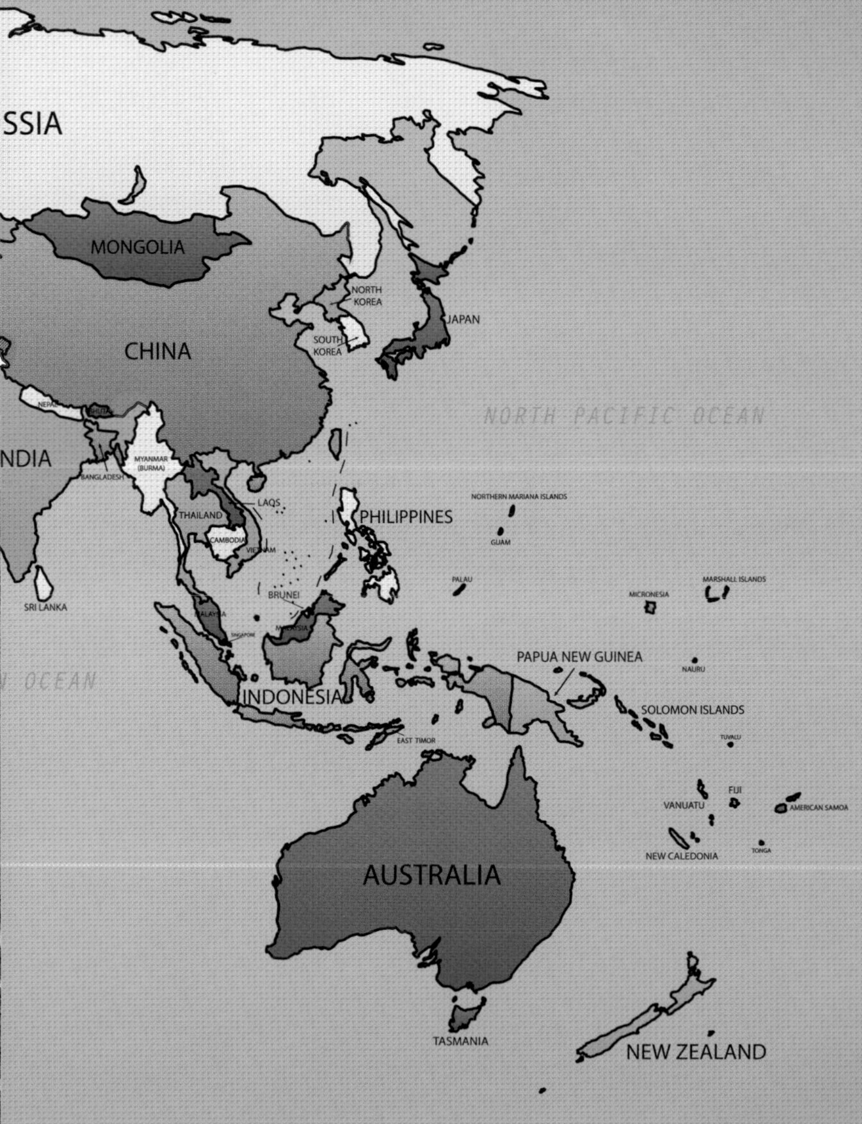

WHICH COUNTRY IS THE **SMALLEST?** TOUCH TO FIND OUT!

WHICH COUNTRY IS THE **BIGGEST?** TOUCH TO FIND OUT!

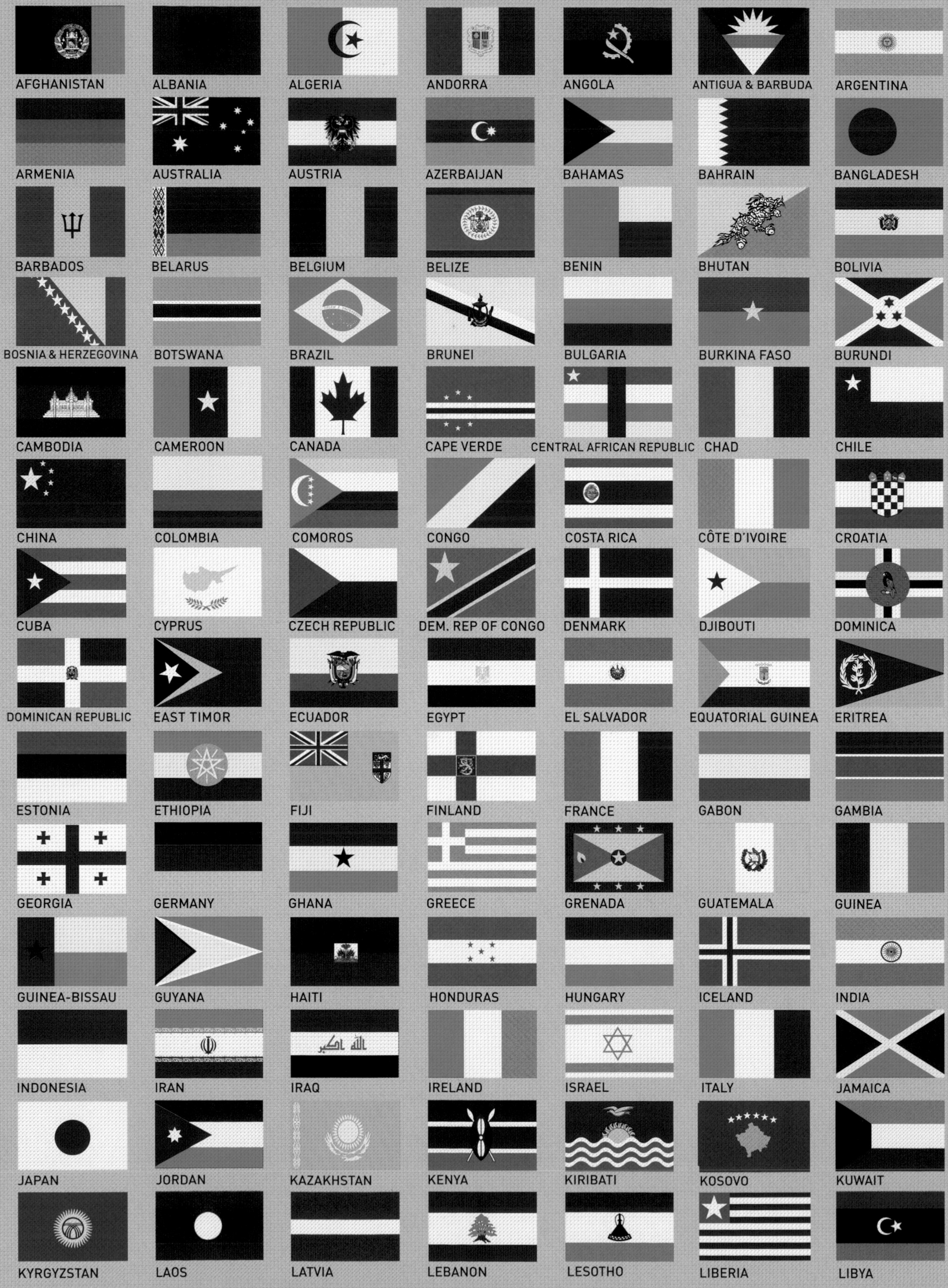
AFGHANISTAN
ALBANIA
ALGERIA
ANDORRA
ANGOLA
ANTIGUA & BARBUDA
ARGENTINA
ARMENIA
AUSTRALIA
AUSTRIA
AZERBAIJAN
BAHAMAS
BAHRAIN
BANGLADESH
BARBADOS
BELARUS
BELGIUM
BELIZE
BENIN
BHUTAN
BOLIVIA
BOSNIA & HERZEGOVINA
BOTSWANA
BRAZIL
BRUNEI
BULGARIA
BURKINA FASO
BURUNDI
CAMBODIA
CAMEROON
CANADA
CAPE VERDE
CENTRAL AFRICAN REPUBLIC
CHAD
CHILE
CHINA
COLOMBIA
COMOROS
CONGO
COSTA RICA
CÔTE D'IVOIRE
CROATIA
CUBA
CYPRUS
CZECH REPUBLIC
DEM. REP OF CONGO
DENMARK
DJIBOUTI
DOMINICA
DOMINICAN REPUBLIC
EAST TIMOR
ECUADOR
EGYPT
EL SALVADOR
EQUATORIAL GUINEA
ERITREA
ESTONIA
ETHIOPIA
FIJI
FINLAND
FRANCE
GABON
GAMBIA
GEORGIA
GERMANY
GHANA
GREECE
GRENADA
GUATEMALA
GUINEA
GUINEA-BISSAU
GUYANA
HAITI
HONDURAS
HUNGARY
ICELAND
INDIA
INDONESIA
IRAN
IRAQ
IRELAND
ISRAEL
ITALY
JAMAICA
JAPAN
JORDAN
KAZAKHSTAN
KENYA
KIRIBATI
KOSOVO
KUWAIT
KYRGYZSTAN
LAOS
LATVIA
LEBANON
LESOTHO
LIBERIA
LIBYA

LIECHTENSTEIN LITHUANIA LUXEMBOURG MACEDONIA MADAGASCAR MALAWI MALAYSIA

MALDIVES MALI MALTA MARSHALL ISLANDS MAURITANIA MAURITIUS MEXICO

MICRONESIA MOLDOVA MONACO MONGOLIA MONTENEGRO MOROCCO MOZAMBIQUE

MYANMAR NAMIBIA NAURU NEPAL NETHERLANDS NEW ZEALAND NICARAGUA

NIGER NIGERIA NORTH KOREA NORWAY OMAN PAKISTAN PALAU

PANAMA PAPUA NEW GUINEA PARAGUAY PERU PHILIPPINES POLAND PORTUGAL

QATAR ROMANIA RUSSIA RWANDA SAINT KITTS AND NEVIS SAINT LUCIA SAINT VINCENT AND THE GRENADINES

SAMOA SAN MARINO SÃO TOMÉ AND PRÍNCIPE SAUDI ARABIA SENEGAL SERBIA SEYCHELLES

SIERRA LEONE SINGAPORE SLOVAKIA SLOVENIA SOLOMON ISLANDS SOMALIA SOUTH AFRICA

SOUTH KOREA SOUTH SUDAN SPAIN SRI LANKA SUDAN SURINAME SWAZILAND

SWEDEN SWITZERLAND SYRIA TAJIKISTAN TANZANIA THAILAND TOGO

TONGA TRINIDAD AND TOBAGO TUNISIA TURKEY TURKMENISTAN TUVALU UGANDA

UKRAINE UNITED ARAB EMIRATES UNITED KINGDOM UNITED STATES URUGUAY UZBEKISTAN VANUATU

VATICAN CITY VENEZUELA VIETNAM YEMEN ZAMBIA ZIMBABWE

POPULATION

The world population is distributed unevenly around the globe. Sixty percent of the world's people in 2013 lived in Asia. Africa had 15.5 percent of the total, followed by Europe with 10.4 percent. South America, Central America, and the Caribbean together had 8.6 percent. Five percent of the world's people lived in North America. The final 0.5 percent lived in Oceania (including Australia and New Zealand).

With a population of more than 8 million, New York City is the largest city in the United States and one of the world's largest as well. Its metropolitan area has a population of almost 19 million.

World population (1700–2000) and population projections (2000–2100)

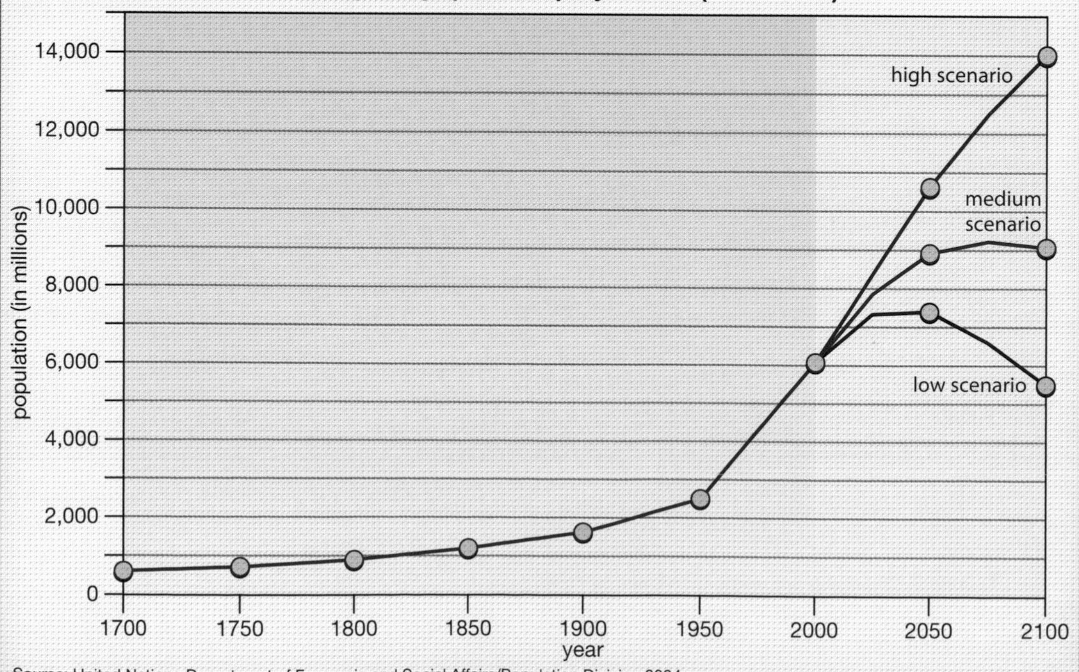

Source: United Nations Department of Economic and Social Affairs/Population Division 2004

Most of the growth in the world population has taken place in the modern era. The time required for the world population to reach its first billion stretched through all of human prehistory into the early 1800s. The second billion was added by 1930, and the 3-billion mark was reached by 1960. The fourth, fifth, sixth, and seventh billions were added by 1974, 1990,1999, and 2011.

Shanghai, China

In 2012 the most densely populated continent by far was Asia. Within continents, there are often significant differences in density from region to region and from country to country.

Mongolia

Earth's population: more than 7 billion people

POPULATION GAME

YES

Two Asian countries, China and India, account for 37 percent of the total world population.

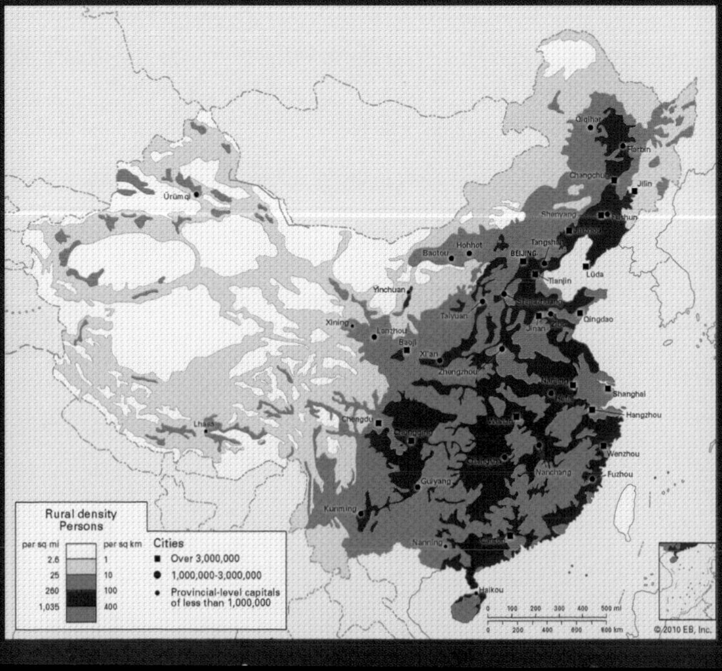

NO

In 2012 the most sparsely populated continent was Australia.

Sydney, Australia

Great Victoria Desert, Australia

AGRICULTURE

There is a great range in agricultural production around the world. Some countries, using high technology and advanced methods, produce more through agriculture than they need or can use, while others—underdeveloped and poorer—never produce enough to sustain their populations. Trying to produce enough food to keep up with the ever-increasing global population is probably agriculture's biggest challenge. By 2030 an estimated additional two billion people will need to be fed, using the same fragile land and water resources that we have now.

World food production has doubled since 1950. Because of the accelerated agricultural productivity, it has been estimated that about one-fifth to one-third of the world's farmable topsoil is being eroded at a rate that will seriously undermine future productivity.

Today, about 1.3 billion, or about one in five, people are farmers. Most of them struggle along as **subsistence** farmers.

Fully half the population of the world depends on rice for fundamental, daily nutrition.

ECONOMICS

An economy is the wealth-producing segment of society. A society creates wealth by producing **goods** and **services**. All the companies producing a particular kind of product or service are grouped together in what is known as an industry. Industries that make things are called manufacturing industries. Industries that sell services are called service industries.

Germany has the largest economy in Europe and one of the largest economies in the world. It has long been an industrial powerhouse and a leading exporter of manufactured goods. Services form the largest sector of the economy.

Record Holders

United States
China
India
Japan
Brazil
Australia

Coal-mining site in China

The forests that cover almost half of Canada's land area supply large wood and paper industries.

THE NATURAL WORLD

The continent of North America is richly endowed with natural resources, including great mineral wealth, vast forests, immense quantities of freshwater, and some of the world's most fertile soils.

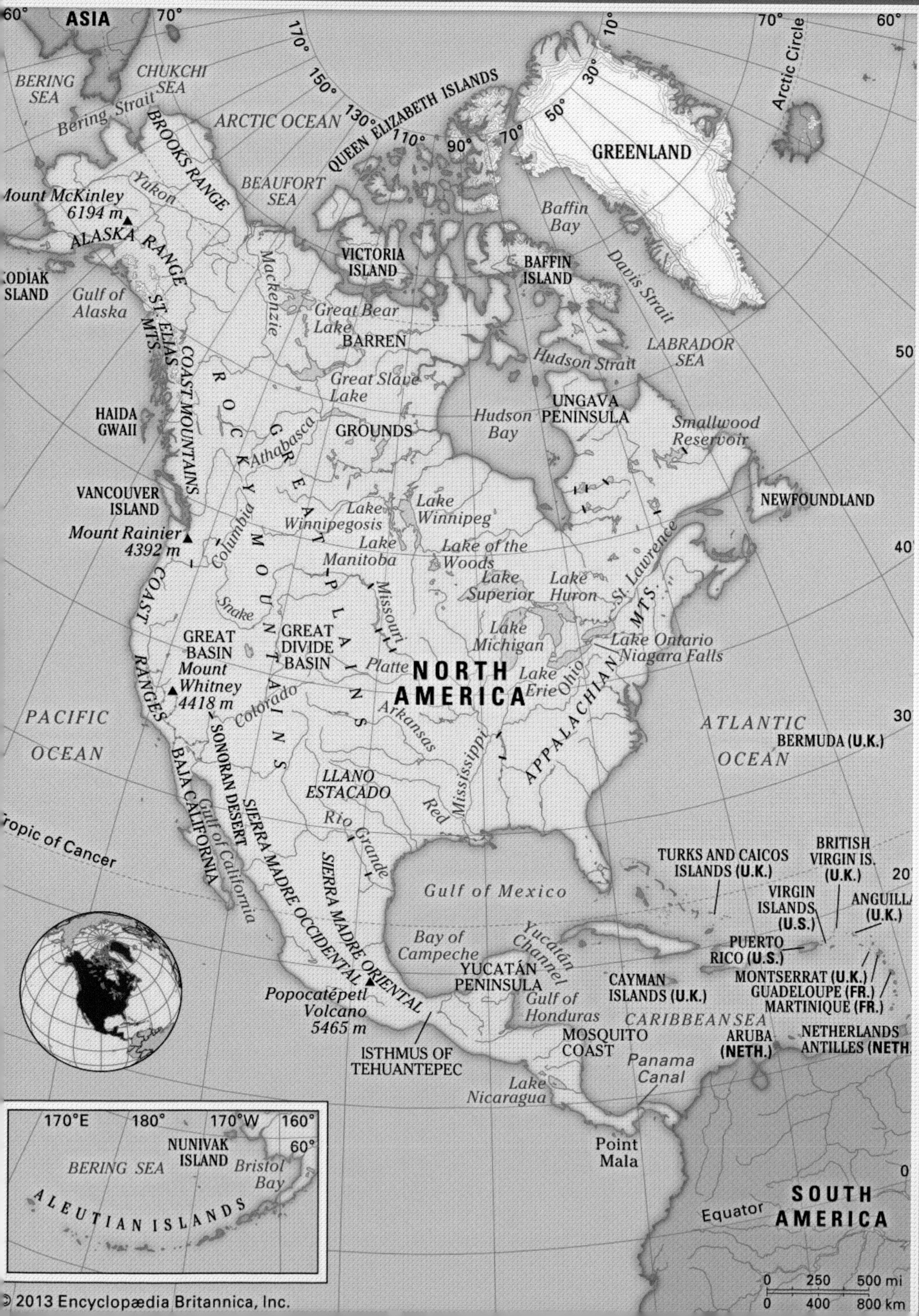

FIND IT!

NORTH AMERICA'S LAND AREA:
9,355,000
SQUARE MILES
(24,230,000 square kilometers)

Which of these animals can be found in the wild in **NORTH AMERICA?**

Lake Superior is the deepest as well as the largest of the Great Lakes.

Death Valley is the lowest point in the Western Hemisphere.

The Mississippi River is one of the longest in the world.

The great center of the continent is dominated by corn and soybeans; beef cattle, pigs, and dairy cattle; and feed crops.

At least 20 volcanoes in Central America are currently active.

NORTH AMERICA THE COUNTRIES

DID YOU KNOW?

POPULATION

LARGEST COUNTRY: CANADA

3,855,103 square miles (9,984,670 square kilometers)

Canada, the United States, and Mexico make up the largest part of the continent of North America. The countries of Central America also are part of the continent, and several islands, including the West Indies and Greenland, are associated with North America. It is third in size and fourth in population among Earth's continents.

COUNTRY FACTS

MOST POPULOUS COUNTRY: UNITED STATES 316,498,000

Mexico City is the oldest city in North America, a continuation of the Aztec capital of Tenochtitlán, founded in about 1325.

Costa Rica is known for its strong commitment to the environment and for protecting its numerous national parks.

NORTH AMERICAN FOODS

A district within the city of Los Angeles, California, Hollywood served as the production center of the U.S. motion-picture industry for more than 30 years.

How long is the border between Canada and the United States?

AMAZING NORTH AMERICA

Situated between the state of New York and the province of Ontario, Niagara Falls is one of the most spectacular natural wonders on the North American continent.

The tall, carved logs called totem poles were erected by prominent people among certain Northwest Coast Indians.

IS IT FOUND IN NORTH AMERICA?

THE TALLEST TREE IN THE WORLD

THE TALLEST BUILDING IN THE WORLD

THE LARGEST SPANISH-SPEAKING COUNTRY IN THE WORLD

True or False?

T F

The ruined ancient Mayan city of Chichén Itzá is located in southeastern Mexico, in the state of Yucatán. Maya peoples founded Chichén Itzá in about the 6th century AD.

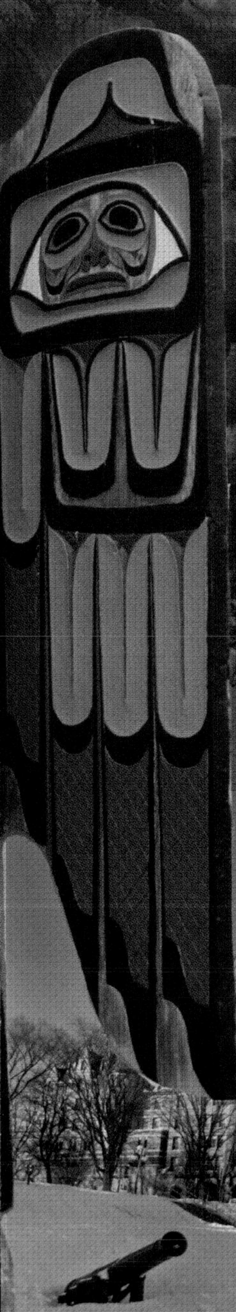

The United States is known to have some 40 species of bats.

The Grand Canyon in Arizona is a 277-mile (446-kilometer) gorge cut through high plateaus by the Colorado River.

Old Faithful, Yellowstone National Park, Wyoming, U.S.A.

Quebec is the only walled city in North America north of Mexico.

The streamertail hummingbird, Jamaica's national bird

THE NATURAL WORLD

South America has an amazing array of physical features and climates, especially in the Andes Mountains, where both tropical and glacial conditions can be experienced within miles of each other.

SOUTH AMERICA'S LAND AREA: 6,875,975 SQUARE MILES
(17,808,695 square kilometers)

AMAZON ANIMALS QUIZ

YES

NO

Beginning in the high Andes Mountains in Peru, the Amazon and its tributaries flow some 4,000 miles (6,400 kilometers) to the Atlantic.

Chile's Atacama Desert is one of Earth's driest places. It sometimes gets no rain for years.

A vast semiarid plateau that covers nearly all of the southern portion of mainland Argentina, Patagonia is approximately 260,000 square miles (673,000 square kilometers) in area.

Llamas are important as transport animals in the Andes Mountains.

Brazil has large amounts of iron, bauxite, columbium-tantalum ores, manganese, tin, gold, and clay, as well as diamonds and other gems.

The diversity of higher plant life in a rainforest is unrivaled by that in any other terrestrial habitat in the world.

SOUTH AMERICA

THE COUNTRIES

South America consists of 12 countries plus an overseas department of France called French Guiana. The continent extends over tropical rainforests, marshes and salt lakes, plains, deserts, and immense highlands.

WHICH COUNTRY?

SOUTH AMERICA'S POPULATION:
nearly 400 million people

DID YOU KNOW?

POPULATION

LARGEST COUNTRY: BRAZIL
3,287,956 square miles (8,515,767 square kilometers)

The Andes Mountains of Peru feature the ruins of many cities built by the Inca people. The most famous of these is Machu Picchu.

Fronted by miles of beaches, the city of Rio de Janeiro, Brazil, is set among the remnants of a once-vast tropical forest that still blankets much of its dramatic mountain backdrop with greenery.

The Andean music of indigenous communities blends syncopated reed flutes, panpipes, drums, and *charangos* (rustic guitars).

Which South American country is the world's leading producer of emeralds?

Among the most spectacular sights in South America are the Iguazú Falls. They are located on a stretch of the Iguazú River that forms the boundary between Brazil and Argentina.

The highest government seat in the world is La Paz, Bolivia. It lies between 10,650 and 13,250 feet (3,250 and 4,040 meters) above sea level.

STUNNING SOUTH AMERICA

This bird is Chile's national bird. What is it?

Rio de Janeiro's Sambadrome is a low-lying complex that provides classroom space for public schools and also serves as the stadium for viewing the samba parades during the annual Carnaval festivities.

Capoeira is an Afro-Brazilian blend of martial arts and dance.

At 12,500 feet (3,810 meters) above sea level, Lake Titicaca is the world's highest lake navigable to large vessels.

The Pampas, or plains, are the homeland of the famous Argentine gaucho, or cowboy.

This mask is found in the Gold Museum in Bogotá, Colombia.

WHO ARE THE LAMOIDS?

alpaca

vicuña

guanaco

llama

GAME

These Peruvian children stand with their alpacas.

THE NATURAL WORLD

A land of extremes and contrasts, Asia is the largest and the most populous continent on Earth. It has the highest mountains and most of the longest rivers, highest plateaus, and largest deserts and plains of all the continents.

FIND IT!

ASIA'S LAND AREA:

more than 17 million square miles (44 million square kilometers)

Orangutans are native to the tropical rainforest on the islands of Borneo and Sumatra.

The Mongolian word *gobi* means "waterless place," and it has become the name for a large desert and semidesert region of Central Asia.

These brown bears live on Russia's Kamchatka Peninsula.

Baikal seal

Lake Baikal is the deepest and oldest freshwater lake in the world.

ASIA: THE COUNTRIES

Asia is home to some of the world's oldest cultures. It has some of the poorest as well as some of the richest countries in the world.

DID YOU KNOW? POPULATION

Which Country?

The army of magnificent life-size terra-cotta statues of men and horses discovered in the early 1970s in the tomb of an emperor who died in 210 BC provide some indication of the long history of Chinese sculpture.

This Indonesian orchestra is called a gamelan.

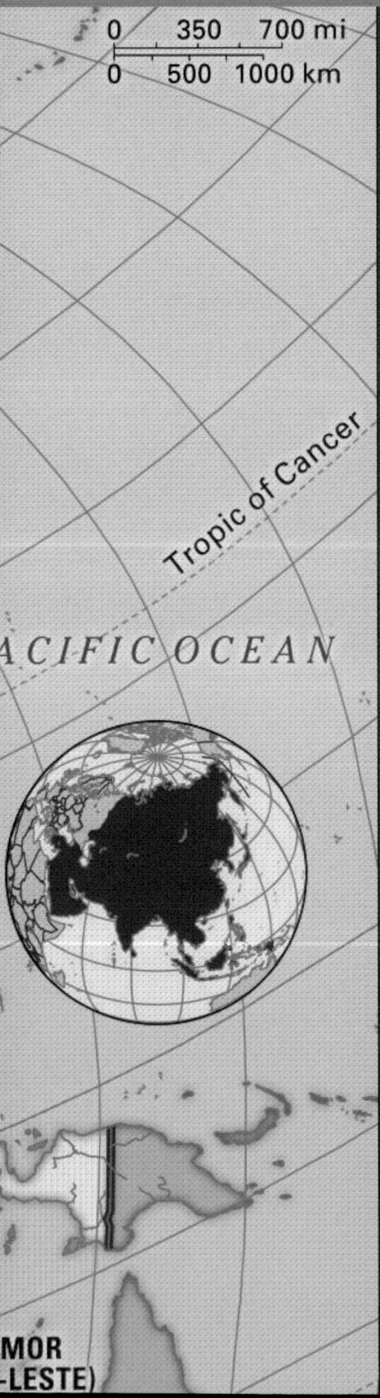

ASIA'S POPULATION: MORE THAN 4 BILLION

LARGEST COUNTRY:
RUSSIA
6,601,700 square miles (17,098,200 square kilometers)

WORLD'S MOST POPULATED COUNTRY:
CHINA
1,357,388,000

Burj Khalifa, a mixed-use skyscraper in Dubai, United Arab Emirates, is the world's tallest building.

ASTONISHING ASIA

One of the largest engineering land building projects ever carried out is the Great Wall of China. Originally a defensive system, it is today a major tourist attraction and a national symbol of China.

Sejong the Great ruled Korea from 1419 to 1450.

Petra was an ancient city located in what is now southwestern Jordan.

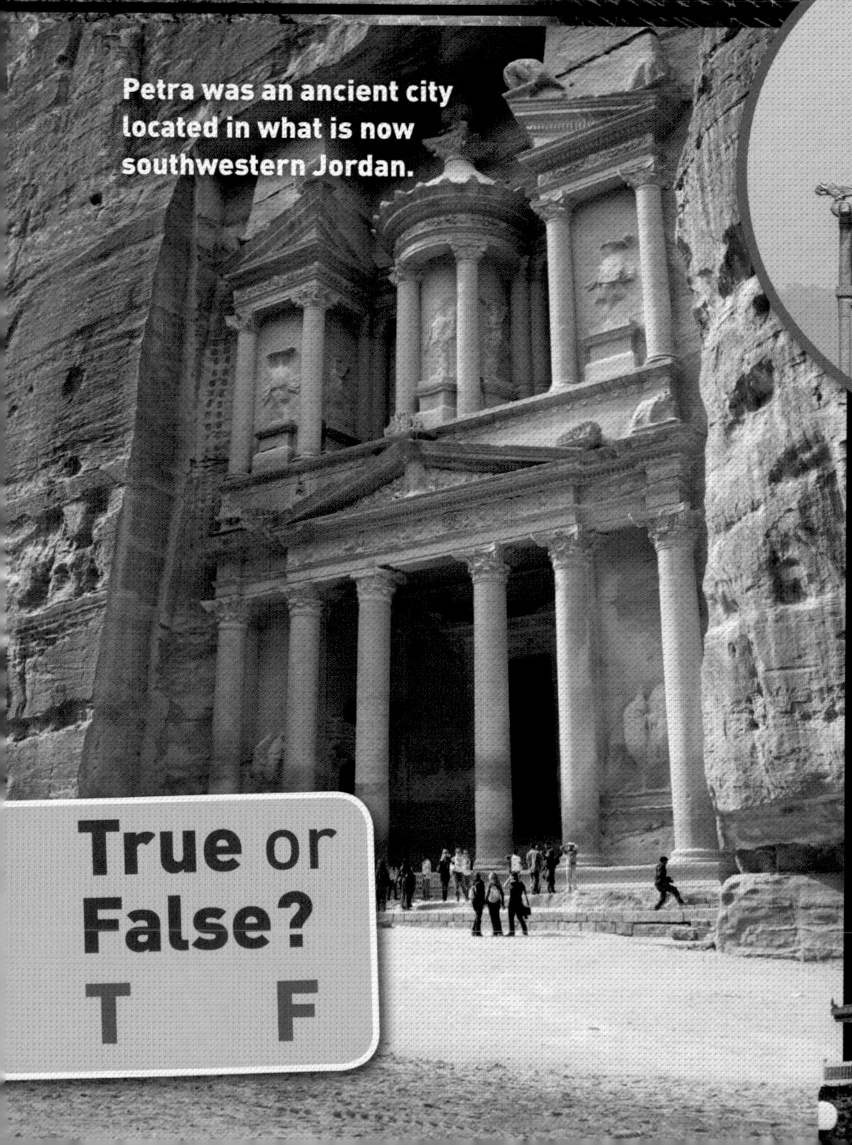

Throughout the Buddhist countries of Asia, holidays are celebrated to commemorate the life and teachings of the Buddha.

True or **False?**

T F

The Taj Mahal is a mausoleum in India. It was built for the favorite wife of Shah Jahan, who was the Muslim ruler of India's Mughal Empire from 1628 to 1658.

Historical records of tamed Asian elephants date to the Indus Valley civilization of the 3rd millennium BC.

Kyrgyzstan's large rural population maintains a traditional lifestyle. Most live in yurts.

Uzbekistan is one of the world's largest cotton producers.

The population of Tokyo's metropolitan area: 36,507,000

THE NATURAL WORLD

HIGHS AND LOWS

Europe is the second smallest continent on Earth, after Australia. It is the western part of the enormous Eurasian landmass, containing Europe and Asia.

How **LARGE** is Europe?

WATERWAYS

The Caspian Sea is the largest inland sea in the world. The area of the Caspian Sea is approximately 149,200 square miles (386,400 square kilometers).

Founded in 1584, Arkhangelsk was the first port of the Russian Empire to conduct trade with England and later with other countries.

WHAT IS THIS FOOD?

The sunniest place in Europe is the Greek island of Rhodes. Rhodes records about 3,480 hours of sunlight annually.

One of the best-known mountains in the Alps, the Matterhorn is located near the Swiss-Italian border. Several thousand people attempt to climb the Matterhorn each year, and a high-altitude glacier allows skiing on the mountain year-round.

EUROPE: THE COUNTRIES

Europe is made up of more than 45 independent countries. Most Europeans live in cities.

CURRENCY QUESTIONS
YES NO

LARGEST COUNTRY ENTIRELY IN EUROPE: UKRAINE

233,062 square miles (603,628 square kilometers)

Europe's population is more than 700 million

DID YOU **KNOW?**

POPULATION

The Balkan country of Yugoslavia existed from 1929 to 2003, as three succeeding federations. A state cobbled together out of many different South Slav peoples with long, separate histories, it was strained by nationalist pressures from its inception.

France's extensive areas of rich soils, combined with generally moderate climates and vast extents of flat to gently rolling land, have long made agriculture a mainstay of the economy.

Portugal is the world's leading producer of a material produced from this tree. What is it?

The organization for the economic and political integration of Europe known as the European Union (EU) was officially created on November 1, 1993. In practice, however, the union traces its origins back to 1950, and it has continued to grow in the 21st century. EU members are sovereign countries that have control over their own basic economic and political affairs, yet they have agreed to follow several EU laws and standards, including treaties regulating regional and world trade, the free movement of citizens within the EU, environmental regulations, and security and law enforcement agreements.

EXPLORE EUROPE

When the French government was organizing the Centennial Exposition of 1889, the noted bridge engineer Alexandre-Gustave Eiffel was asked to design and build a structure to symbolize the occasion.

Venice is world renowned as a city of canals and bridges.

ARCHITECTURE ID

On April 26, 1986, a catastrophic nuclear reactor meltdown and explosions occurred at the Chernobyl nuclear power plant in Ukraine, 80 miles (130 kilometers) north of Kiev.

This statue of the Little Mermaid is a beloved symbol of Copenhagen, Denmark.

Windsor Castle is the largest inhabited castle in the world.

Each of Romania's regions has its own costumes, art, and customs.

Nomadic reindeer herding was the traditional way of life for most **Sami** until the late 20th century.

The Greek theaters were magnificent structures. Fifteen or twenty thousand spectators sat in bleacherlike tiers built on a hillside in an arc around the acting and dancing space, called the orchestra.

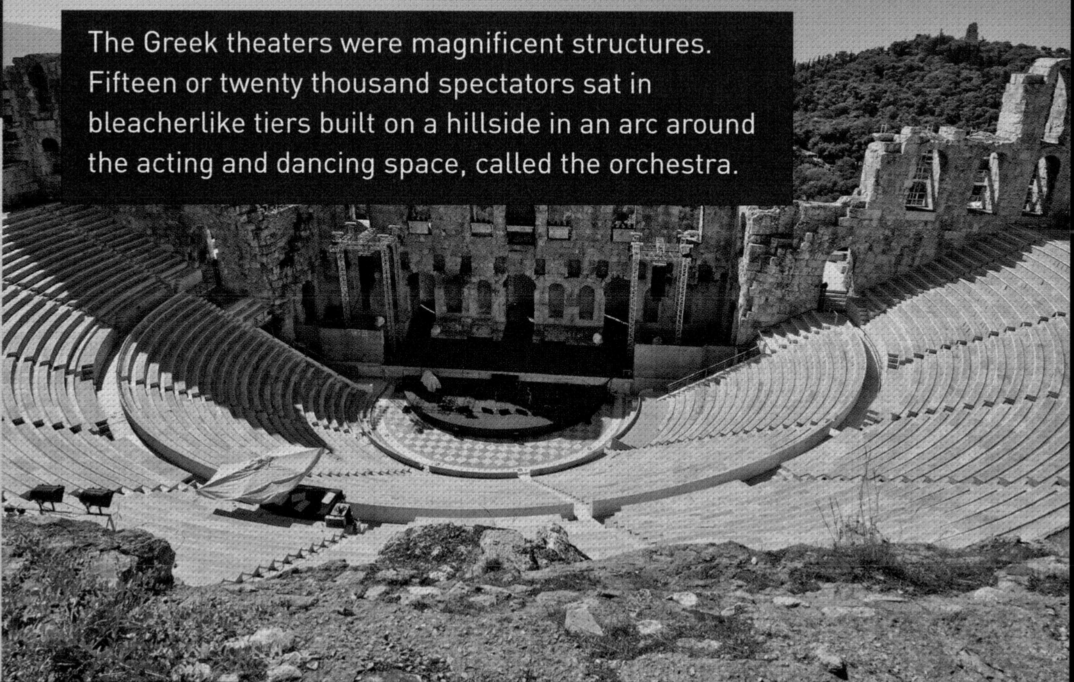

THE NATURAL WORLD

Africa is the second largest landmass in the world, after Eurasia, and its area is more than three times that of the United States. Geologically, Africa is one of the oldest continents. Because of its age, Africa has undergone erosion for hundreds of millions of years. Most of the mountains have been worn away, and today much of the continent is a rolling plateau ranging between 500 and 4,500 feet (150 and 1,400 meters) above sea level.

AFRICA'S LAND AREA: 11,724,000 SQUARE MILES (30,365,000 square kilometers)

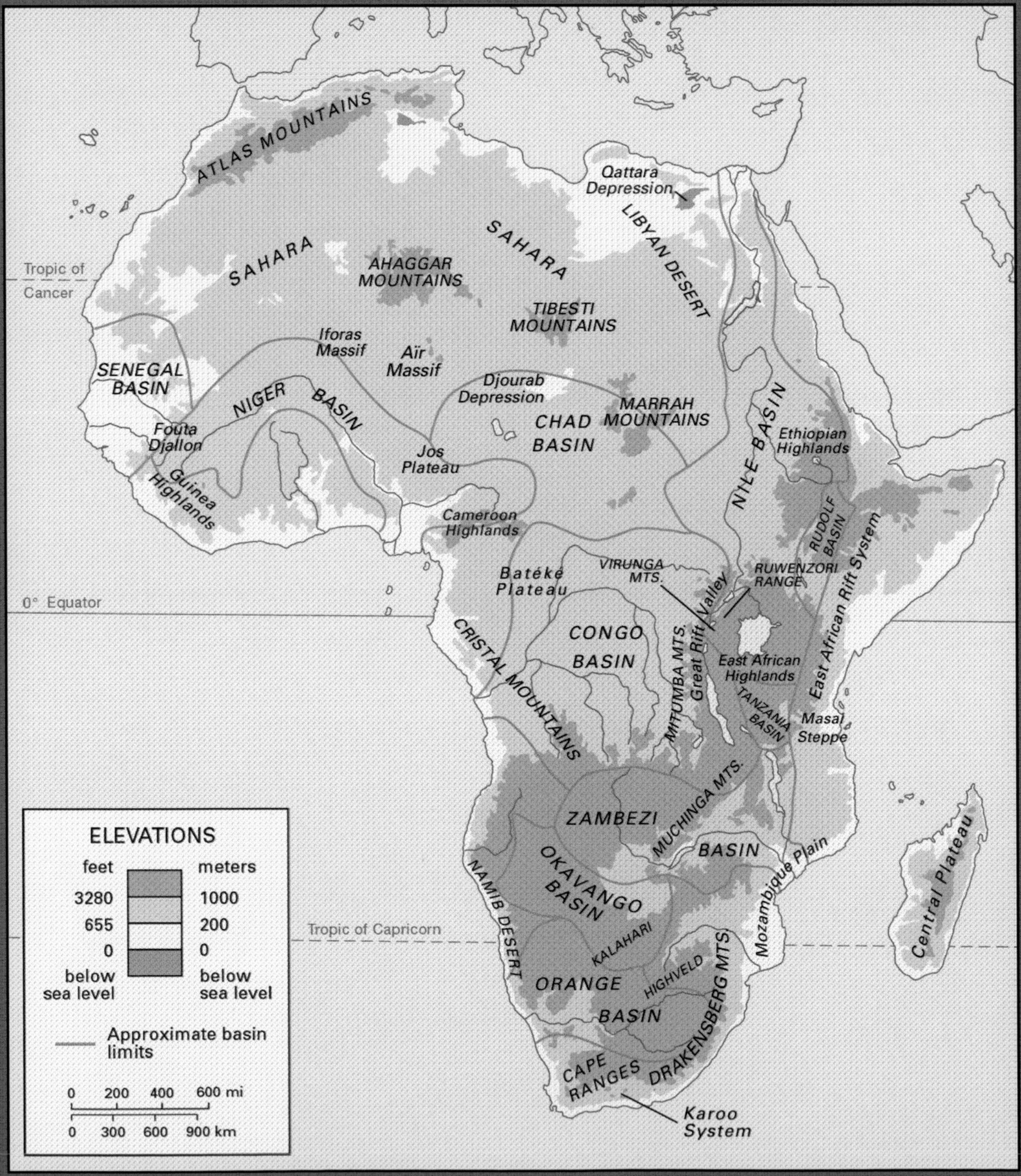

SUMMER MONSOON WINDS

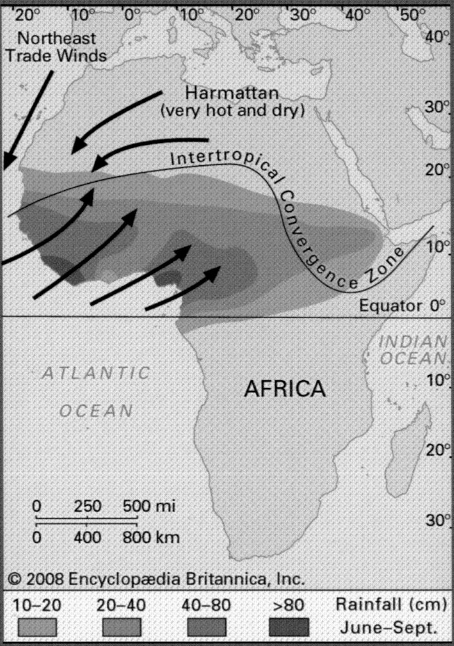

WINTER MONSOON WINDS

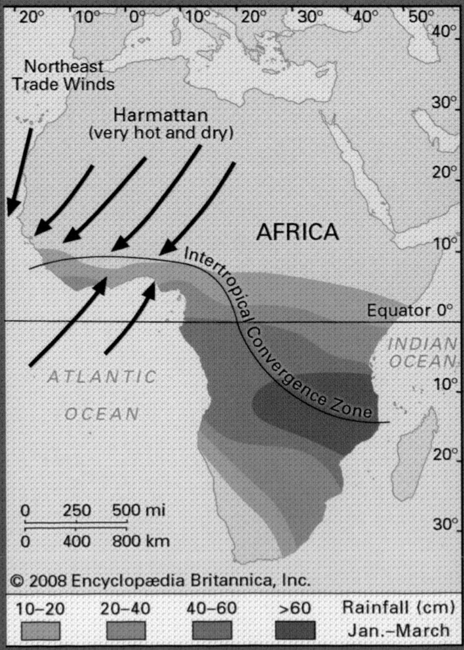

In parts of West and East Africa, the climate is affected by the seasonal **monsoon winds.**

Many of the world's essential minerals, including copper, gold, and uranium, are mined in Africa.

Madagascar is the home of some 50 species of lemur, a tree-dwelling primate.

Ngorongoro Crater is an extinct volcanic caldera in Tanzania. It is thought to have formed about 2.5 million years ago from a large active volcano whose cone collapsed inward after a major eruption, leaving the present vast, unbroken caldera as its chief remnant.

The equatorial regions of Africa have year-round rainfall.

This animal is found in the Sahara. What is it?

Name it!

AFRICA
THE COUNTRIES

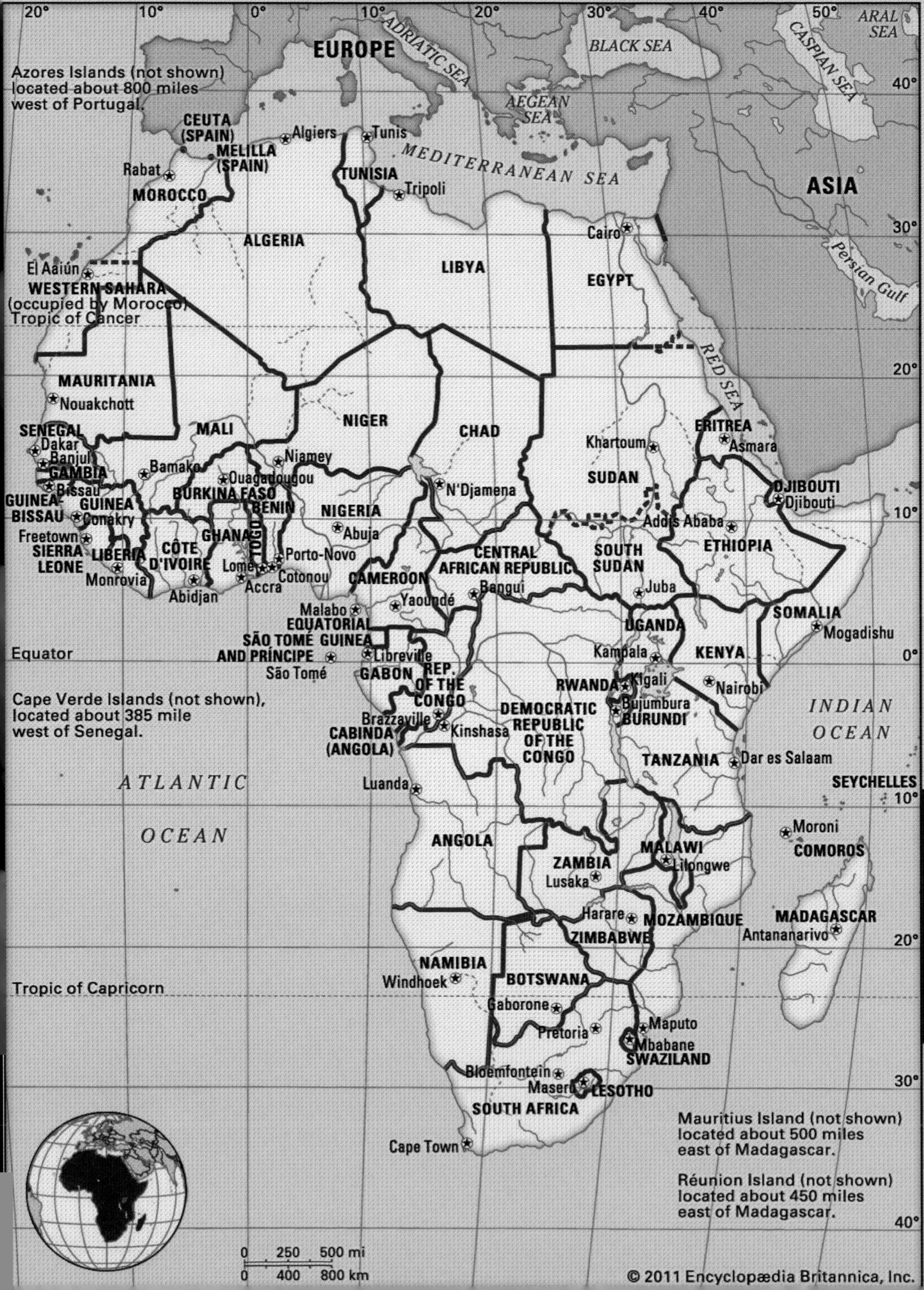

There are more than 50 independent countries in Africa and on the islands off its coasts. Most of Africa was controlled by European countries from the19th century until after World War II. After these colonies became independent countries, some enjoyed peace and economic growth. But many struggled with such problems as poor political leadership, civil war, poverty, inadequate educational systems, and disease.

MOST POPULOUS COUNTRY: NIGERIA
174,508,000

LARGEST COUNTRY: ALGERIA
919,595 square miles (2,381,741 square kilometers)

DID YOU **KNOW?**

POPULATION

LANGUAGE FAMILIES AND LANGUAGES OF AFRICA

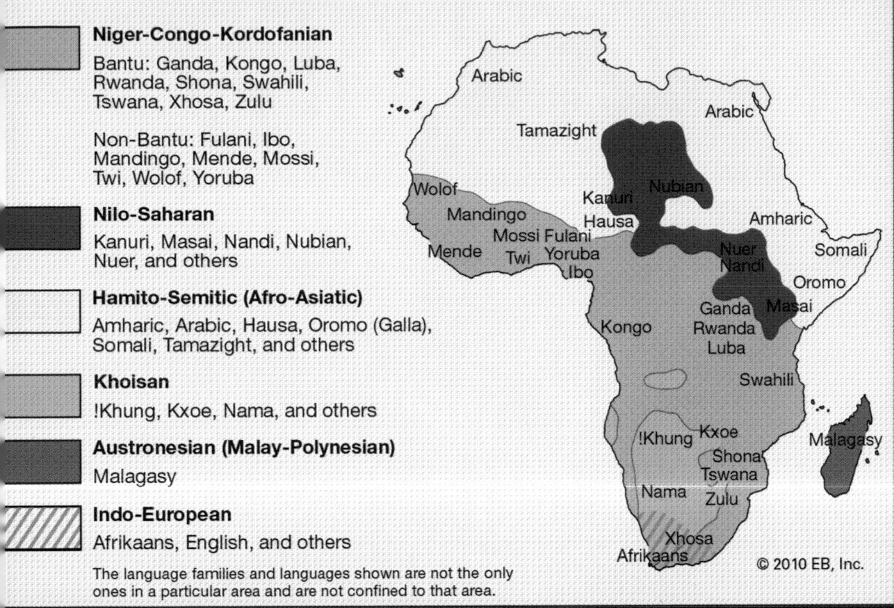

800 to 1,000 languages are spoken in Africa today.

MATCH THE CAPITAL

RABAT **NAIROBI**

DAKAR **CAIRO**

PRETORIA

During the days of the Roman Empire, people learned to use the camel for travel in the Sahara. The camel provided a perfect mount for the Tuareg, a pastoral Berber people who dominated much of the central Sahara.

Once, Kente cloth was only made for the political leaders of the Ashanti Empire (now southern Ghana).

This mud-walled mosque in Djenné, Mali, was designated a World Heritage site in 1988.

The ruins of Great Zimbabwe attest to the stone-working skills of the region's inhabitants, the ancestors of the present-day Shona people.

AWESOME AFRICA

Did you know? Africa is widely recognized as the birthplace of human beings.

Mount Kilimanjaro is made of three major extinct volcanoes. Its central cone, the snow-clad Kibo, is the youngest of the volcanoes.

An obelisk from the ancient kingdom of Aksum, in what is now Ethiopia

One of the world's mightiest waterfalls, Victoria Falls is on the border between Zambia and Zimbabwe.

Some of the earliest human remains have been found at Tanzania's Olduvai Gorge.

In Africa, poaching is a major danger to wildlife conservation. In order to stop poaching, African governments have created huge national parks that serve as wildlife sanctuaries. Some cover thousands of square miles.

FIND THE FOOD SOURCE

Ethiopia's capital Addis Ababa is the highest city in Africa.

Lagos, Nigeria, is one of the largest cities in the world, with the metropolitan area population estimated at more than 11 million people.

A traditional mask made by the Yoruba people

THE NATURAL WORLD

Thousands of islands scattered across the Pacific Ocean are grouped together under the name of Oceania. The region is generally divided into three major areas: Melanesia, Micronesia, and Polynesia. Sometimes a fourth area, called Australasia, is also considered to be a part of Oceania. This area includes Australia, New Zealand, and nearby islands. Australia is the only continent occupied entirely by a single country. It is the flattest, most arid, and least populated of the inhabited continents.

True or False?
T F

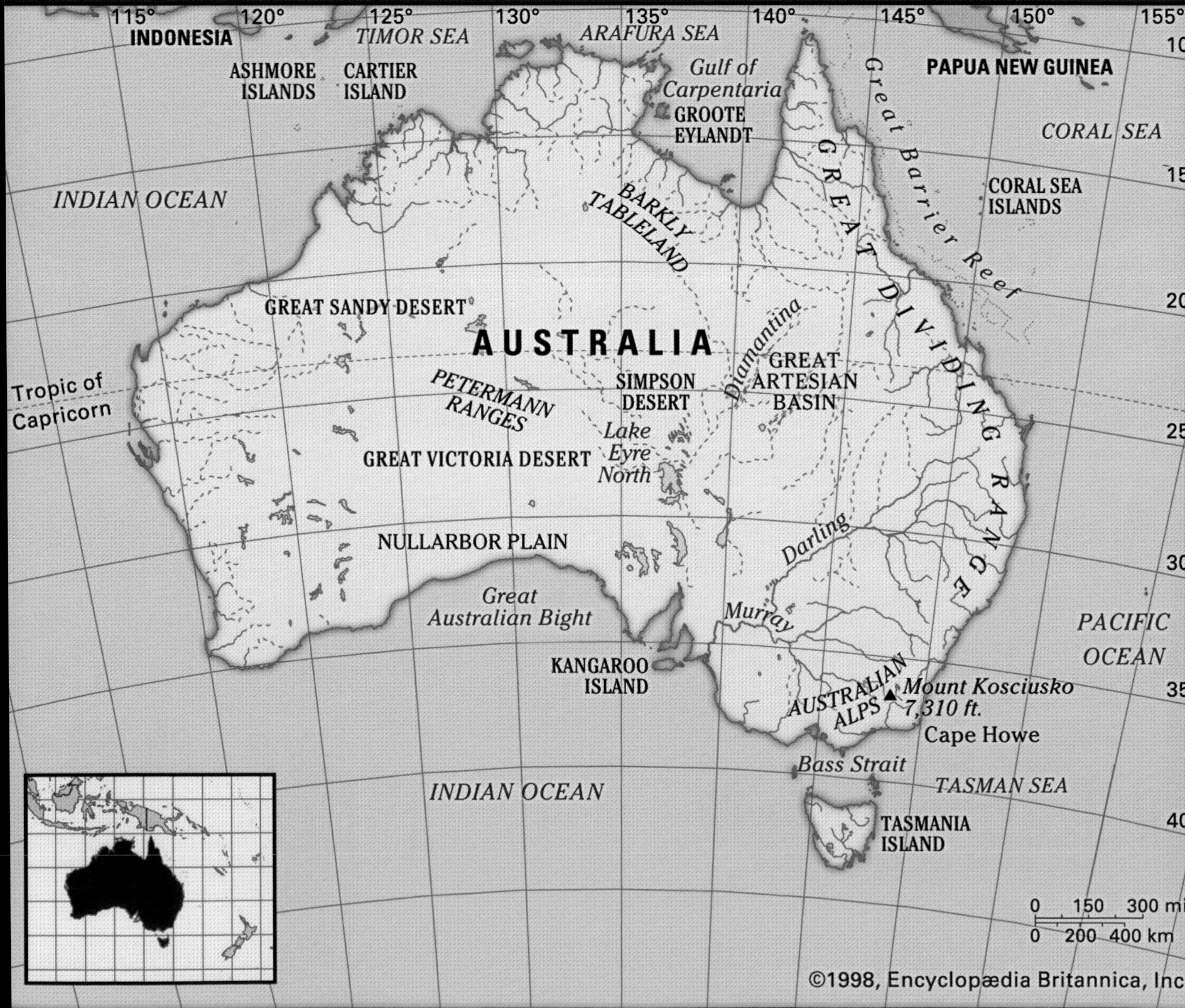

How big is Oceania?

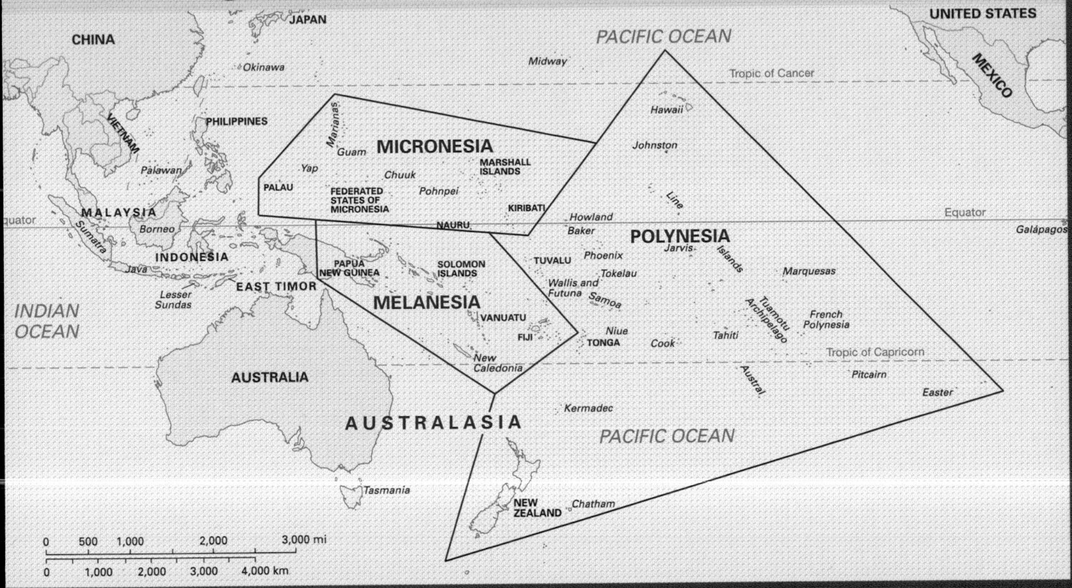

The geographic region Oceania includes roughly 10,000 islands in the Pacific Ocean.

The larger islands of Fiji are of volcanic origin and are mountainous. The smaller ones are coral **atolls**.

Despite its name, the Great Barrier Reef is not a single **reef**. It actually includes some 2,900 reefs.

As a result of millions of years of isolation from Asia, Australia has many plant and animal species that are found nowhere else in the world, including the platypus.

One of Australia's most famous landmarks, Uluru/ Ayers Rock is a giant mass of weathered sandstone.

New Zealand's landscapes exhibit spectacular contrasts, including steep fjords, rocky and sandy shores, glaciers, rugged mountains, lush subtropical forests, and miles of verdant pastures and cropland.

AUSTRALIA AND OCEANIA
THE COUNTRIES

Although it is not a large continent, Australia is the world's sixth largest country, after Russia, Canada, China, the United States, and Brazil. Yet only some 20 million people inhabit this vast area. Some of the islands of Oceania are crowded with people, but others are total wilderness. About 14 million people live in the region of Oceania, nearly three-quarters of them in New Zealand and Papua New Guinea.

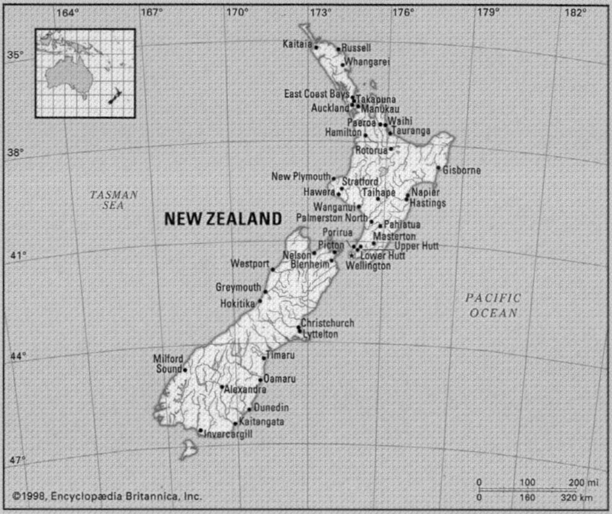

WHAT DO YOU KNOW?
POPULATION

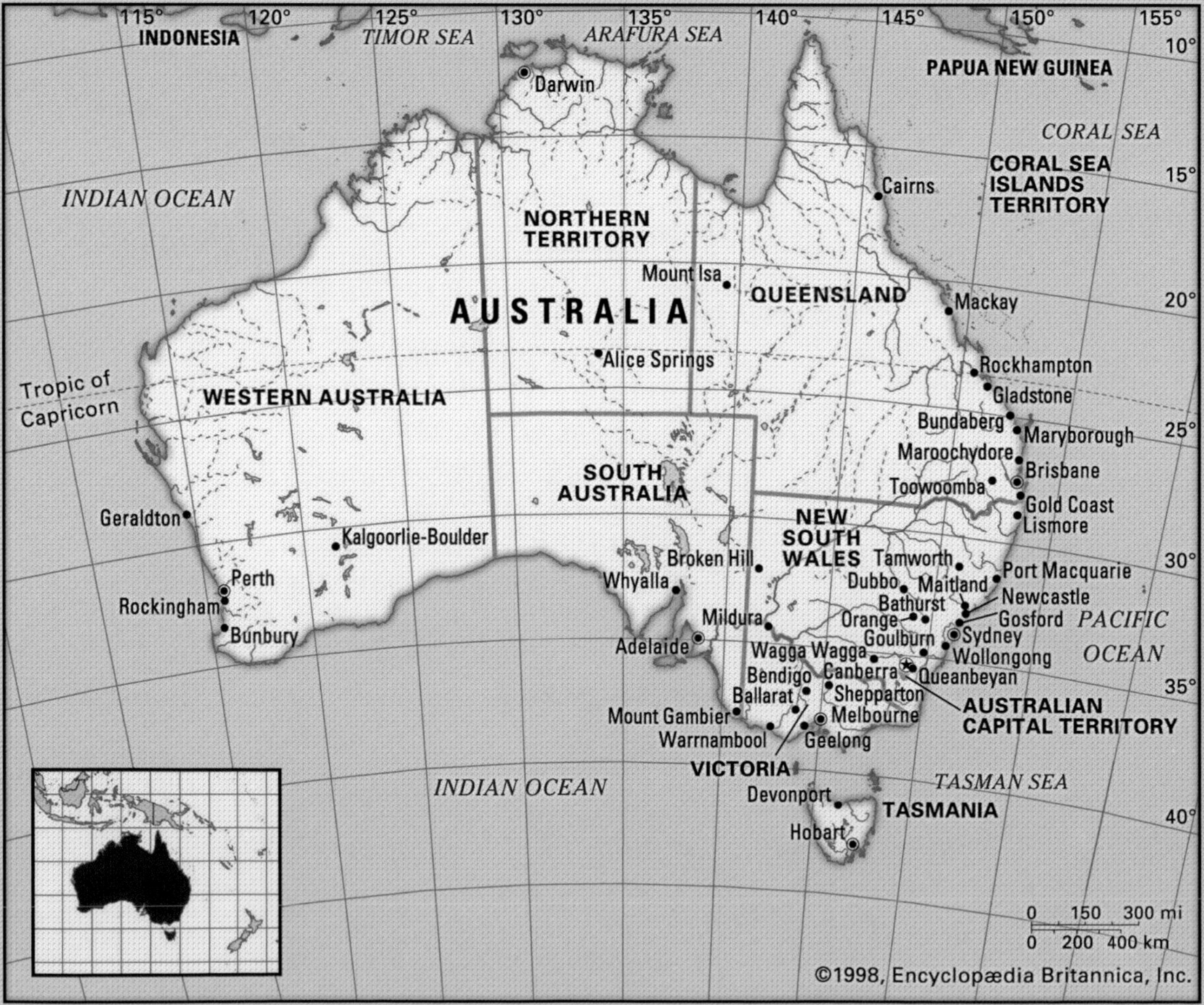

SMALLEST COUNTRY: NAURU
8.2 square miles (21.2 square kilometers)

For thousands of years, Aborigines in Australia have created art for spiritual, ritual, and other purposes, including pleasure.

Four of Samoa's nine islands are inhabited. Apia, shown here, is the capital and largest town.

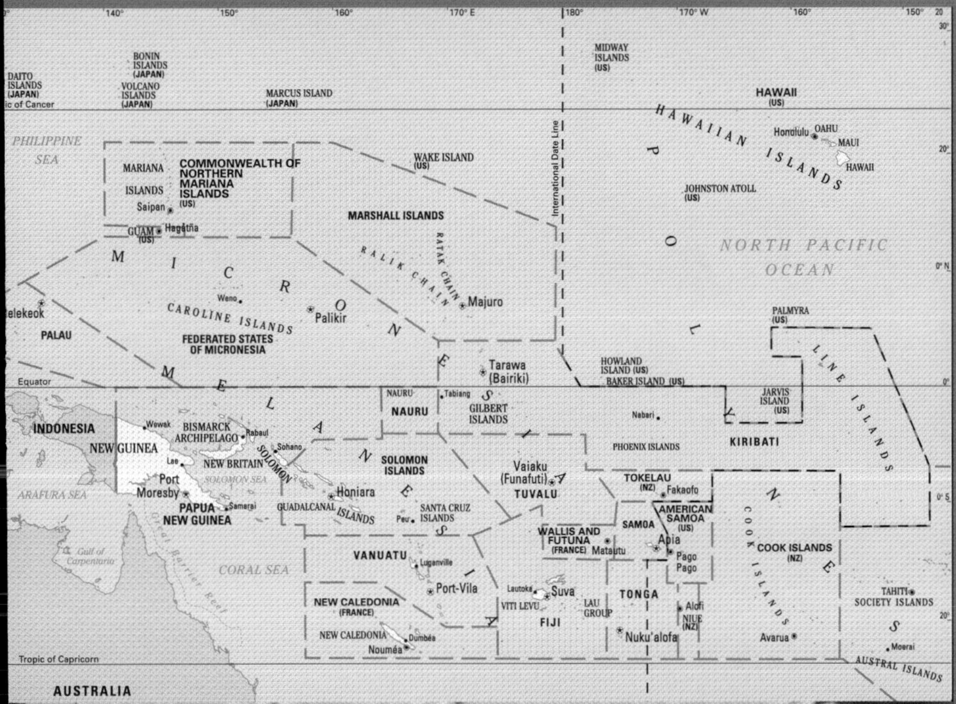

WHICH COUNTRY?

More than 60 percent of all Australians live in the metropolitan areas of the eight state and territorial capitals.

Most of New Zealand's native plant and animal species are not found anywhere else, including this lizard, the tuatara.

DIVING DOWN UNDER

Did you know? Australia is the only continent where venomous snakes outnumber the nonvenomous ones.

How many languages are spoken in Papua New Guinea? Touch the photo to find out!

AUSTRALIAN ANIMALS

grey kangaroo

wallaby

echidna

dingo

Tasmanian devil

koala

Lyrebirds can mimic the sounds of more than 20 other songbirds.

Before people arrived in New Zealand, no land mammals reached the isolated islands apart from a few species of bats. In the absence of predatory mammals, New Zealand was a paradise for birds, including many flightless species.

New Zealand was first settled by the ancestors of the Maori, perhaps in the late 1200s.

Australia is home to several hundred species of eucalyptus trees, which are often called eucalypts or gums.

Famous for the gleaming white Sydney Opera House and its picturesque waterfront, Sydney is the largest and oldest city in Australia.

Australia has many remarkable caves.

ANTARCTICA

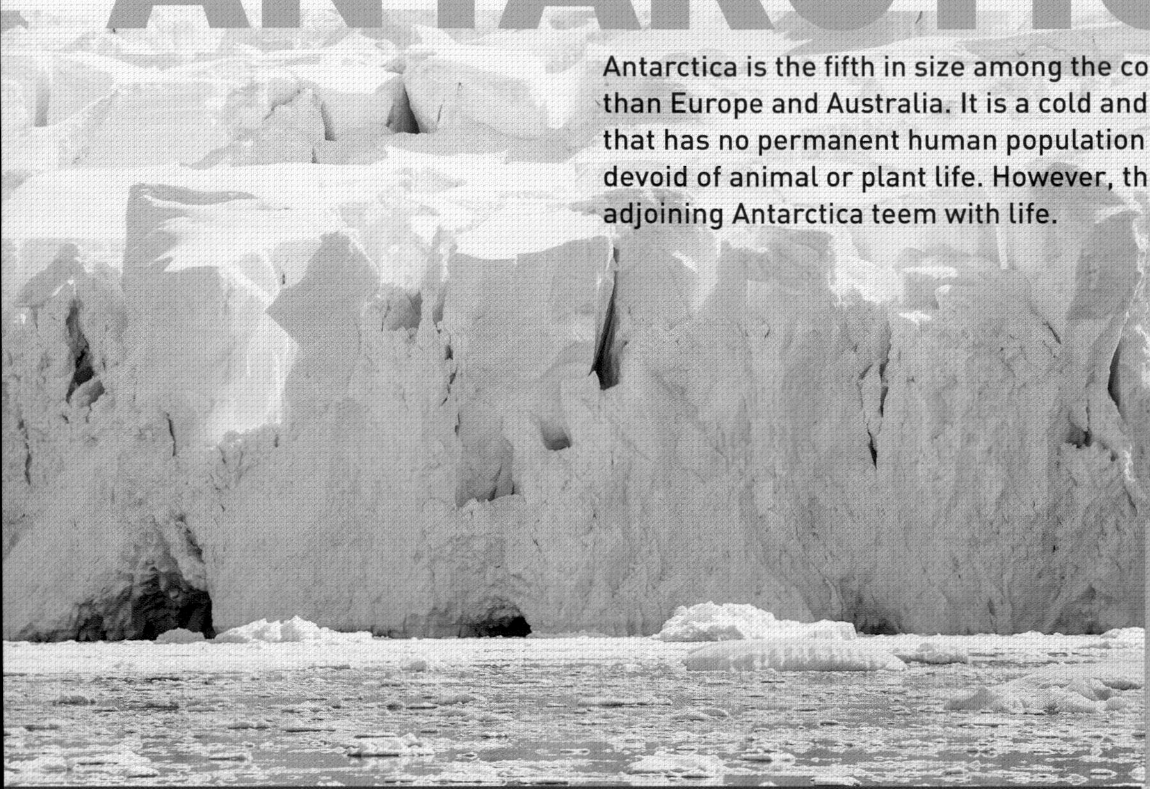

Antarctica is the fifth in size among the continents, larger than Europe and Australia. It is a cold and forbidding land that has no permanent human population and is almost devoid of animal or plant life. However, the oceans adjoining Antarctica teem with life.

An ice sheet covers nearly all of Antarctica. This ice sheet contains 90 percent of the world's ice and 70 percent of the world's freshwater.

Beginning in the early 20th century several explorers set out to reach the South Pole. Roald Amundsen reached it first, in December 1911.

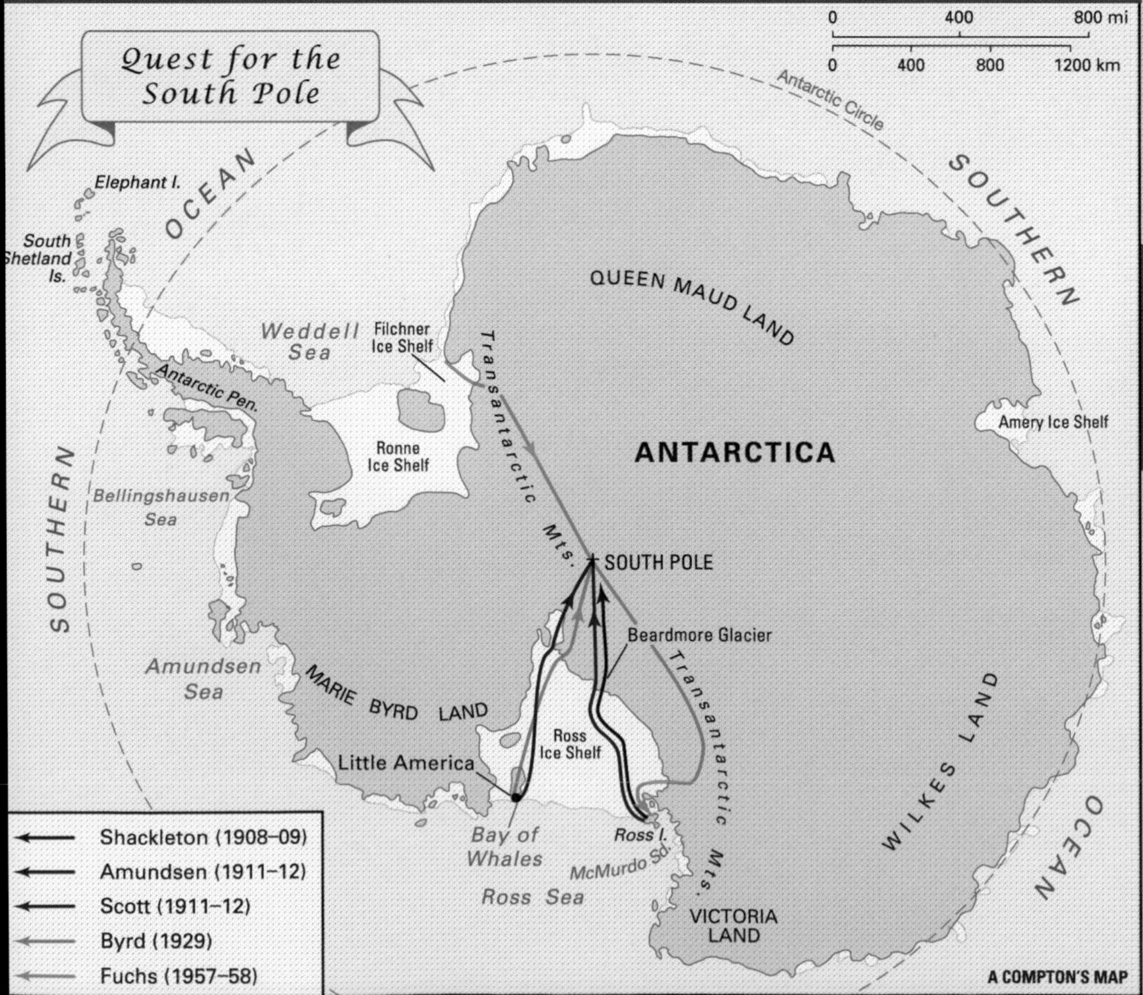

DID YOU KNOW?

YES NO

Was Antarctica always cold?

Where is the South Pole?

World's lowest temperature: −128.6° F (−89.2° C)

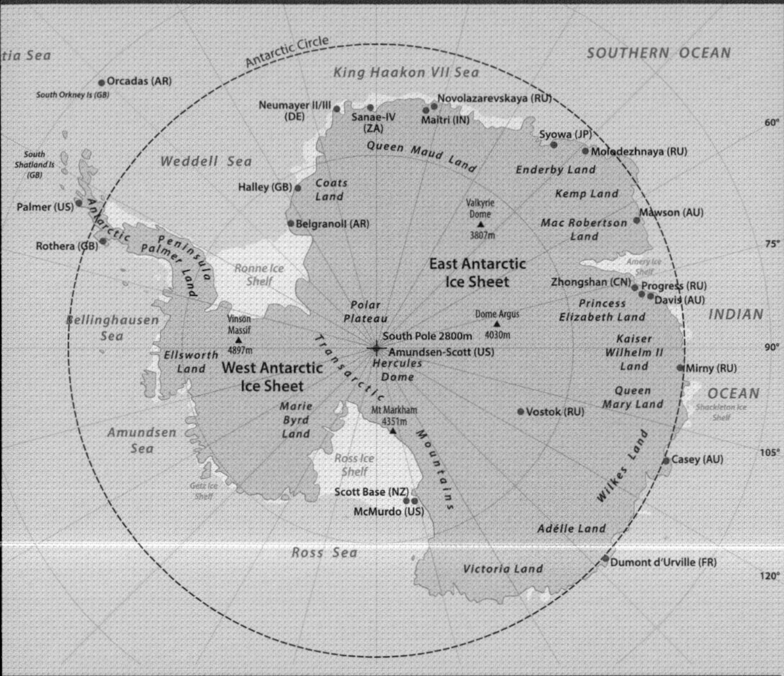

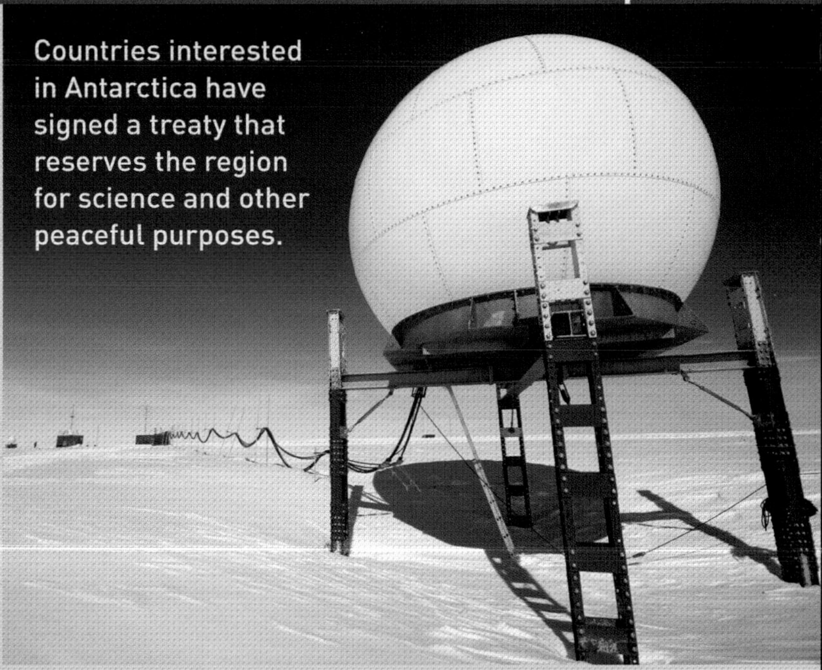

Countries interested in Antarctica have signed a treaty that reserves the region for science and other peaceful purposes.

Sea mammals native to Antarctica include seals, porpoises, dolphins, and whales. Four species of seals, including the leopard seal shown here, breed almost exclusively in the Antarctic.

The most important single member of the Antarctic marine food chain is the krill. This crustacean looks like a small shrimp and exists in huge numbers.

About 45 species of birds live south of the Antarctic Convergence. Two penguin species—the emperor and the Adélie—are distributed widely around the entire coastline.

OUR EARTH

If you could walk around the Earth, following the Equator, how long would you walk?

7,926 miles
(12,756 kilometers)

24,902 miles
(40,075 kilometers)

How far have humans drilled into the Earth?

7.62 miles
(12.26 kilometers) deep

40 miles
(64.37 kilometers) deep

The majority of the people of the world live on this percent of Earth's surface.

10 percent

40 percent

What is the average temperature on Earth?

59° F (15° C)

69° F (20° C)

About how many kinds of animals live on Earth?

1.3 million

8 million

How far is Earth from the sun?

8 million miles
(12 million kilometers)

60 million miles
(96 million kilometers)

93 million miles
(150 million kilometers)

Mt. Everest is the world's highest mountain. What is the second highest?

K2, near the Pakistan/China border

Kilimanjaro, in Tanzania

One of the most common elements in Earth's crust is:

Carbon

Gold

Iron

Oxygen

Silicon